illustration Now! 3

Ed. Julius Wiedemann

illustration
Now! 3

TASCHEN

Contents
Inhalt / Sommaire

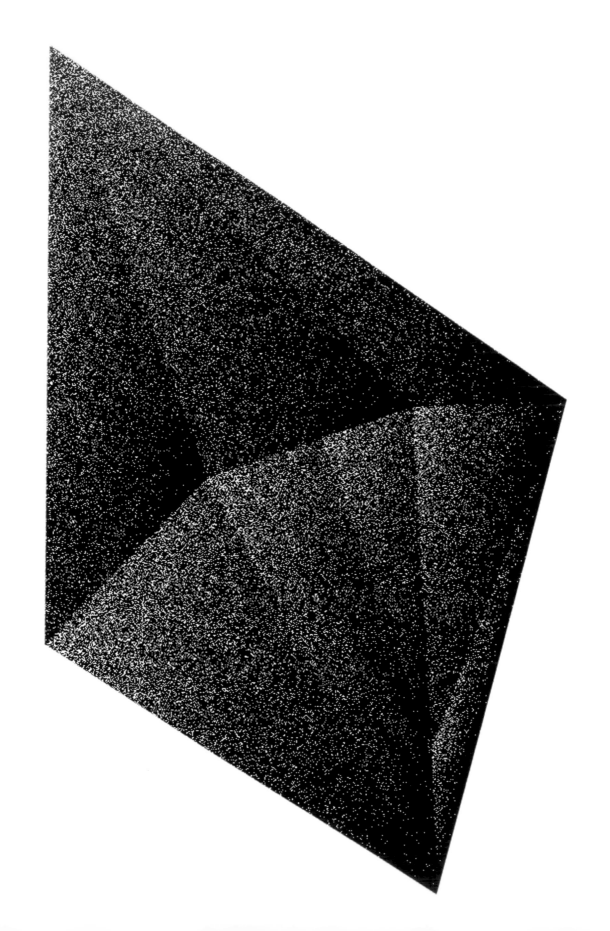

Foreword

by Julius Wiedemann

When we first started with *Illustration Now!* back in 2005 we could see that there was a real need to publish a comprehensive showcase of what was happening in the contemporary illustration scene, taking into consideration the fact and the evidence that this form of expression had been going through a period of major transformation, both in the way it is produced and in the way people perceive it. The boom in recent years in gallery exhibitions and special events planned specifically to show illustration as a form of art have taken the world by storm, not to mention the expansion of media using illustration on walls and in public spaces, in clothing, electronic devices, cars, and many other outlets. From toy art to editorials, from advertising to store decoration, from package design to fashion, our perception was that more people than ever were now appreciating illustration.

The United States is still undoubtedly the most important country in the illustration market, with New York being its largest hub. As well as being home to an incredible number of artists, the United States has always attracted amongst the best talents from around the world, and for a long time it was also, probably, the only place where they might be compensated accordingly for the effort and genius of their work. However, with the increasing facility to work remotely, and to produce, communicate, and share ideas using digital tools, these possibilities have now spread to other parts of the globe. Important players such as the United Kingdom, Germany, Canada, France, and Japan have become more representative in the international arena, whilst new players such as Spain, China, and Argentina continue to grow stronger in the quantity and quality of their contributions.

This renaissance in illustration and its varied applications can also be attributed to the new communication and distribution possibilities we have today, specifically those which facilitate its access to a wider audience, thus generating a pathway to a greater appreciation of really high-quality work. Now that both audience and illustrators have access to more reference material and production means, the bars have certainly been raised, and all kinds of techniques, styles, cultural references, and approaches to ideas can be more fully explored.

One of the most difficult things in putting a book like *Illustration Now!* together is choosing the right criteria for selection. What sets *Illustration Now!* apart from other showcases is that we have always featured a range of 150 illustrators, never repeating a single one in each subsequent edition, thus making each new volume a discovery and a reference that doesn't lose its value. The final selection, in our case, is based upon a combination of factors which, first of all, praise quality, but also the diversity the illustrated world offers to our eyes. This diversity is represented in every aspect of the selection process, such as in the illustrator's country of origin, years of experience, techniques, use of colors, styles, awards received, participation in exhibitions, along with many other factors.

For my part, I have consistently had the good fortune to work with the eagle eyes of one of the greatest experts in the world, Steven Heller, who today, after years at the *New York Times*, is co-chair of the MFA Designer as Author program at the School of Visual Arts, New York. Once again, we have set out to create another unique collection of 150 of the most talented illustrators and their works, hoping this third volume is used as those previously as a major resource by agencies, art directors, studios, media firms, artists, students, and illustration connoisseurs alike.

Vorwort

von Julius Wiedemann

Als wir 2005 den ersten Band von *Illustration Now!* herausbrachten, war der Bedarf an einer umfassenden Darstellung aktueller Strömungen in der Illustratorenszene für uns deutlich erkennbar. Das Buch sollte anhand von Beispielen der Tatsache Rechnung tragen, dass diese Ausdrucksform sowohl im Hinblick auf die Produktionsweise als auch auf die Rezeption eine Phase tiefgreifender Veränderungen durchlaufen hatte, anhand von Beispielen Rechnung tragen. Der Trend der vergangenen Jahre, Illustrationen mittels Galerieausstellungen und Special Events als Kunstform zu etablieren, hat die Welt im Sturm erobert, ganz abgesehen von der immer breiteren medialen Nutzung von Illustrationen an Hauswänden und im öffentlichen Raum, bei Bekleidung, elektronischen Geräten, Autos und vielen anderen Produkten. Von künstlerisch gestalteten Spielzeugen bis hin zu Veröffentlichungen, von der Werbung bis hin zur Gestaltung von Geschäftsräumen, vom Verpackungsdesign bis hin zur Mode – unserem Eindruck nach wussten noch nie so viele Menschen Illustrationen zu schätzen.

Die USA sind zweifelsohne immer noch der wichtigste Markt für Illustrationen, und New York steht dabei deutlich im Mittelpunkt. Dort ist nicht nur eine unglaubliche Vielzahl von Künstlern beheimatet, sondern die USA haben stets die besten Talente aus aller Welt angezogen; für lange Zeit war es wahrscheinlich auch der einzige Ort, wo sie dem Aufwand und der Genialität ihrer Arbeit entsprechend vergütet wurden. Doch weil es zunehmend einfacher wird, auch an abgelegenen Orten zu arbeiten, zu produzieren, zu kommunizieren und mittels digitaler Instrumente Ideen auszutauschen, bieten sich diese Möglichkeiten auch in anderen Teilen der Welt. Wichtige etablierte Akteure wie Großbritannien, Deutschland, Kanada, Frankreich und Japan sind international immer besser vertreten, während aus den Ländern, die wie etwa Spanien, China und Argentinien erst seit Kurzem auf sich aufmerksam gemacht haben, etwa, immer mehr und qualitativ hochwertigere Arbeiten auf den Markt kommen.

Diese Renaissance der Illustration und ihrer vielfältigen Anwendungsmöglichkeiten ist auch den neuen Kommunikations- und Distributionswegen zuzuschreiben, die uns heute zur Verfügung stehen und die es uns erleichtern, ein größeres Publikum zu erreichen und dadurch Wege zu größerer Anerkennung und Wertschätzung qualitativ wirklich hochwertiger Arbeiten eröffnen. Jetzt, da Publikum und Illustratoren auf mehr Referenzmaterialien und Produktionswege zugreifen können, sind die Ansprüche natürlich gestiegen, und alle möglichen Techniken, Stile und kulturellen Bezüge können umfassender untersucht werden.

Die Wahl geeigneter Aufnahmekriterien ist eine der schwierigsten Aufgaben bei dem Unterfangen, ein Buch wie *Illustration Now!* zusammenzustellen. Für jeden neuen Band haben wir eine Gruppe von 150 Illustratoren zusammengestellt, von denen keiner zweimal erwähnt wird. Jeder Folgeband bietet somit neue Entdeckungen und ist ein Referenzwerk, das nie seinen Wert verlieren wird; das unterscheidet *Illustration Now!* von anderen Darstellungen. In unserem Fall basiert die endgültige Auswahl auf einer Kombination von Faktoren; in erster Linie stellen wir die Qualität heraus, aber wir berücksichtigen auch die Vielfalt, die uns die Welt der Illustrationen offenbart. Diese Vielfalt prägt jeden Aspekt des Auswahlprozesses, wenn es z.B. um das Herkunftsland der Illustratoren, ihre Berufserfahrung, die Techniken, den Einsatz von Farben und Stilen, die verliehenen Auszeichnungen sowie die Teilnahme an Ausstellungen und um viele weitere Faktoren geht. Ich für meinen Teil hatte jedes Mal das große Glück, unter den Adleraugen eines der weltweit größten Experten arbeiten zu können. Ich spreche von Steven Heller, der heute – nach vielen Jahren bei der New York Times – Mitvorsitzender des *MFA Designer as Author*-Programms der School of Visual Arts in New York ist. Wieder einmal haben wir uns daran gemacht, eine einmalige Sammlung von 150 der talentiertesten Illustratoren und ihrer Arbeiten zusammenzustellen. Wir hoffen, dass diese dritte Ausgabe wie auch schon die Vorgängerbände von Agenturen, Art Directors, Studios, Medienunternehmen, Künstlern, Studenten sowie von Liebhabern und Kennern von Illustrationen als wichtige Quelle genutzt wird.

Préface

par Julius Wiedemann

Lorsque nous avons entrepris *Illustration Now!* en 2005, nous pressentions un réel besoin de voir publier un panorama complet de ce qui se passait sur la scène de l'illustration contemporaine, compte tenu du fait qu'à l'évidence cette forme d'expression venait de traverser une période de profonde transformation, du point de vue de son mode de production comme que de la perception du public. L'explosion, dans les dernières années, des expositions de galerie, ainsi que les manifestations organisées tout spécialement pour montrer l'illustration comme un art à part entière, ont pris le monde par surprise, pour ne rien dire de l'essor de l'illustration comme support médiatique, sur les murs des villes et des espaces publics, dans le domaine l'habillement, de l'électronique et de l'automobile, entre autres. Du « toy art » à l'édition, de la publicité à la décoration de magasin, du design d'emballage à la mode, nous avions le sentiment qu'on ne s'était jamais autant intéressé à l'illustration.

Les États-Unis restent indubitablement le grand pays du marché de l'illustration, avec New York pour plaque tournante. Résidence d'élection d'un incroyable nombre d'artistes, l'Amérique a toujours attiré les meilleurs talents du monde et elle a longtemps été le seul endroit où leurs efforts ainsi que leur génie avaient une chance de se voir récompensés à leur juste valeur. Cependant, comme il est de plus en plus facile de travailler à distance, et de concevoir, communiquer et partager des idées au moyen d'outils numériques, ces possibilités se sont étendues à d'autres parties du globe. D'importants acteurs tels que le Royaume Uni, l'Allemagne, le Canada, la France et le Japon se sont imposés sur la scène internationale, tandis que d'autres, et notamment l'Espagne, la Chine et l'Argentine, continuent de grandir en termes de quantité comme de qualité de leurs contributions.

Ce renouveau de l'illustration et de ses diverses applications peut également être attribué aux nouvelles possibilités de communication et de distribution dont on dispose aujourd'hui, en particulier celles qui contribuent à la faire connaître de plus larges audiences, tout en ouvrant la voie à une meilleure appréciation d'un travail d'une réelle et très haute qualité. Maintenant que public et illustrateurs ont accès à davantage de matériel de référence et de moyens de production, les barrières ont assurément été levées et toutes sortes de techniques, de styles, de références culturelles et d'approches conceptuelles vont pouvoir être explorées plus à fond.

Quand on conçoit un ouvrage tel que *Illustration Now!* l'une des principales difficultés tient au choix de bons critères de sélection. *Illustration Now!* se distingue d'autres compilations en ce que nous avons choisi de toujours y présenter 150 illustrateurs, sans jamais en répéter un seul dans l'édition suivante, faisant ainsi que chaque nouveau volume une découverte et une référence dont la valeur restera entière. Le choix final, dans notre cas, repose sur une combinaison de facteurs qui exaltent, avant tout, la qualité, mais aussi la diversité que le monde de l'illustration offre à nos yeux. Cette diversité est représentée par chaque aspect du processus de sélection : pays d'origine de l'illustrateur, années d'expérience, techniques, emploi des couleurs, styles, récompenses reçues, participation à des expositions, et bien d'autres facteurs.

Pour ma part, j'ai invariablement eu la chance de travailler avec l'aide des yeux de lynx de l'un des plus grands experts du monde, Steven Heller, qui, aujourd'hui, après des années au *New York Times*, est le coprésident du programme de *MFA Designer as Author*, de l'École d'arts visuels de New York. Une fois encore, nous présentons donc un aréopage unique de 150 illustrateurs parmi les plus talentueux, ainsi que leurs travaux, en espérant qu'à l'instar des précédents, ce troisième volume sera précieux aux agences, directeurs artistiques, studios, médias, artistes, étudiants et autres amateurs d'illustration.

Viable and Enviable

by Steven Heller

I should not be so surprised that this is the third edition of *Illustration Now!*, but honestly, I never conceived that there would even be a second volume. The prospect that illustrators had a viable, no less enviable, future was questionable back when volume one was planned. From the perspective of an editorial art director I was convinced that the shrinking of newspapers and magazines, the greater reliance on photography, the over-art direction of art, and the surfeit of those pesky Photoshop collages was cutting into the demand for solid illustration. Advertising was no longer a fertile market and a drought was occurring in the editorial realm that promised to have devastating effects.

But at the risk of sounding too Pollyanna (I prefer being dour), things have changed – for the better in most cases. The editorial well is no longer running dry, and even advertising has begun to show signs of reinvigoration. Moreover, other rich markets and media – from toys to fashion, from animation to video games – are opening up to illustration, or something that looks like it (although some of it blurs the line between commercial and fine art). In conjunction with this sense of optimism, the overarching fear that the computer would kill illustration as we knew and loved it has not come to pass – in fact, the computer has doubtless made illustration more attractive in many ways.

Sure, some of the veterans have left the field for the vagaries of gallery art, and others have been replaced by a newer wave of upstarts, but there are still – as evidenced in volumes I, II, and III – a goodly number of very talented, highly motivated illustrators ready, willing, and able to tackle assignments (sound like a motivational speech?) and entrepreneurially invent products. Just today I met with a young illustrator who had such personal vigor and impressive, raw talent that I wanted immediately to assign him work to do. If this had been just three years ago, I would have been hard-pressed to tell him where to take his work, but now I can rattle off a dozen market venues. I am convinced he has a future.

Every time I say the word "market" I feel a chill go up my spine. I hate the sound and implication of that word. For the longest time I referred to places for illustration as "outlets" not markets. Why taint the process with crass business terminology? Illustrators are artists, right? And by extension, so are art directors who commission (and guide them). In art it is okay to produce for an audience of one. It is okay for the artist to ignore suggestions to alter a work because it is "inappropriate". It is axiomatic that the artist will fall on his or her sword for the integrity of their art. But it is ridiculous not to think of illustration as a business, lest the illustrator be put out of business owing to ignorance. Illustration is definitely a creative commodity and the illustrator provides a service to the customer. The only difference between this and run-of-the-mill consumer-driven products is the fact that illustrators offer more than a mere functional object: they provide visual intelligence, aesthetics, and ideas, and as such are employed for their ability to do so.

When I was fretting over the possibility that illustration was in its final stage, I kept asking myself what could replace it as a means of entertaining, informing, and yes, attracting people? Could illustration really go the way of silhouette cutting or sampler sewing? I don't think so. Too much depends on drawn or painted artwork to allow it to atrophy completely. So here we are deep into *Illustration Now! Volume 3* and there are still numerous illustrators, young and old, worth showcasing not just because they have solid portfolios but because they have earned impressive visible commissions – the enviable kinds that have an effect on our visual culture.

What is also inspiring is the broad range of graphic and conceptual endeavor from so many parts of the globe. Certain styles dominate – neo-Art Nouveau and neo-Deco have seen a curious rise during the past three years, as though an aesthetic reaction to the *art brut* that had held sway during the previous decade. This renewal of ornamental graphic conceits, notably the tendrils and vines that cover everything from T-shirts to book jackets, may owe a debt to software that makes precise rendering and flawless repetition so easy. Or it may have something to do with the increased need to return exemplary craft back to illustration after a decade or more of primitive styling. Although sketchier illustration is still popular, a lighthearted comic tone underscores the majority of illustrations today.

In addition to stylistic trends, conceptual approaches vary greatly and also pleasingly. There may be less overt political commentary in this volume, despite the 2008 American Presidential election, but there is an abundance of visual puns and other thought-provoking ideograms and other mind-jogging imagery. What's more, caricature, which was left for endangered, if not altogether comatose, a decade ago, has returned as both commentary and entertainment.

Yet despite all the striking illustration compiled for this volume, something is missing: the bombshell. The incomparable work by an individual or a group, based on style or concept, that so definitively captures, if not defines, the zeitgeist that it will be forever linked to the time in which it was conceived. Maybe it is too soon to tell. Distance is always useful in judging anything with zeitgeist in the title. Or maybe we are beyond such a phenomenon. As healthy as illustration may be – and I say it is – it is not the most significant of arts. The days when James Montgomery Flagg or Norman Rockwell ruled the popular culture roost are over. Perhaps illustration now (today) is the sum of its parts. If so, then *Illustration Now! Volume 3* may not be a bombshell, but it is a cluster bomb.

"Every time I say the word 'market'
I feel a chill go up my spine.
I hate the sound and implication of that word."

Lebensfähig und beneidenswert

von Steven Heller

Eigentlich sollte ich nicht überrascht sein, dass wir schon beim dritten Band von *Illustration Now!* angekommen sind, aber ehrlich gesagt habe ich mir nicht einmal einen zweiten vorstellen können. Die Aussicht auf eine lebensfähige, geschweige denn beneidenswerte Zukunft für Illustratoren war bei den Planungen für den ersten Band noch recht fragwürdig. Aus der Perspektive des Herausgebers und Art Directors war ich davon überzeugt, dass die Nachfrage nach solider Illustration in Anbetracht eines schrumpfenden Zeitungs- und Zeitschriftenmarktes, eines größeren Zutrauens in die Fotografie, der ausufernden Einmischung von Art Directors in die Kunst und einer Schwemme lästiger Photoshop-Collagen beschnitten würde. Die Werbung war kein schöpferischer Markt mehr, und im Editorial-Bereich breitete sich eine Dürreperiode aus, die verheerende Auswirkungen befürchten ließ.

Doch auch auf die Gefahr hin, wie ein unverbesserlicher Optimist zu klingen (ich bin lieber etwas nüchterner): Die Dinge haben sich geändert – in den meisten Fällen hin zum Besseren. Die redaktionellen Quellen drohen nicht mehr länger zu versiegen, und sogar in der Werbung gibt es Anzeichen für eine Neubelebung. Überdies öffnen sich der Illustration oder dem, was danach aussieht (obwohl einiges die Grenze zwischen Kommerz und schönen Künsten verwischt) andere, ergiebige Märkte und Medien – von Spielzeug bis hin zur Mode, von Trickfilmen und Animationen bis hin zu Videospielen. Dieser Optimismus ist eng damit verknüpft, dass sich die allumfassende Befürchtung nicht bewahrheitet hat, dass Illustrationen, wie wir sie kennen und lieben, durch Computer abgetötet werden könnten. Vielmehr hat der Computer zweifelsohne in mehrfacher Hinsicht dazu beigetragen, dass Illustrationen attraktiver geworden sind.

Sicher, viele Veteranen haben die Branche verlassen und sich den Launen der Galeriekunst ausgesetzt, und andere wurde von einer neuen Welle von Nachrückern ersetzt, aber es gibt – wie die Bände I, II und III zeigen – immer noch viele talentierte, höchst motivierte Illustratoren, die bereit und fähig sind, Aufträge zu übernehmen und unternehmerisch denkend neue Produkte zu erfinden (das klingt wie die Ansprache bei einem Motivationstraining, oder?). Gerade heute traf ich einen jungen Illustrator mit einer derart persönlichen Vitalität und einem solch beeindruckenden, unverbrauchten Talent, dass ich ihm gleich ein paar Aufgaben übertragen wollte. Hätte ich ihn vor drei Jahren getroffen, wäre es mir außerordentlich schwergefallen, ihm zu sagen, wo er Arbeit findet. Aber heute kann ich ihm sofort ein Dutzend Schauplätze nennen, auf denen er seinen Markt finden kann. Ich bin davon überzeugt, dass wir in Zukunft noch von ihm hören werden.

Jedes Mal, wenn ich das Wort „Markt" verwende, läuft es mir kalt den Rücken hinunter. Ich hasse Klang und Implikationen dieses Wortes. Die meiste Zeit habe ich bei den Anwendungsgebieten für Illustrationen von „Abnehmern" gesprochen und nicht von Märkten. Warum sollen wir den schöpferischen Prozess mit krasser Business-Terminologie beflecken? Illustratoren sind doch Künstler, oder? Und im weitesten Sinne gilt das auch für die Art Directors, von denen sie beauftragt (und angeleitet) werden. In der Kunst ist es kein Problem, für ein Publikum zu produzieren, das lediglich aus einer Person besteht. Der Künstler kann problemlos Vorschläge ignorieren, seine Arbeit abzuändern, weil sie „unpassend" sei. Er würde sich grundsätzlich für die Integrität seiner Kunst ins Schwert stürzen. Doch es ist lächerlich, die Illustration nicht als Geschäft zu betrachten, denn sonst fliegt der Illustrator aufgrund seiner Ignoranz aus eben diesem. Illustrationen sind definitiv kreative Erzeugnisse, und der Illustrator bietet dem Kunden eine Dienstleistung. Der einzige Unterschied zwischen diesem und den am Verbraucher orientierten Produkten von der Stange ist der, dass Illustratoren mehr bieten als rein funktionale Objekte: Sie liefern visuelle Intelligenz, Ästhetik und Ideen und werden folglich wegen ihrer Fähigkeit beschäftigt, genau das zu tun.

*„Jedes Mal, wenn ich das Wort ‚Markt‘ verwende,
fühle ich, wie es mir kalt den Rücken hinunterläuft.
Ich hasse seinen Klang und die Implikationen dieses Wortes.“*

Als ich mir Sorgen machte, dass sich die Illustration möglicherweise schon im Endstadium befinde, habe ich mich immer wieder gefragt, was es wohl sein würde, wodurch sie in ihren Möglichkeiten zu unterhalten, zu informieren und, ja, die Aufmerksamkeit der Menschen auf sich zu ziehen ersetzt werden könnte. Ist es wirklich möglich, dass die Illustration den gleichen Weg nehmen wird wie das Silhouettenschneiden oder das Mustersticken? Davon gehe ich nicht aus. Zuviel hängt von gezeichneter oder gemalter Kunst ab, als dass sie vollständig verkümmern könnte. Nun sind wir also mitten drin in *Illustration Now! Volume 3*, und es gibt immer noch zahlreiche Illustratoren, junge und alte, die es wert sind, hier vorgestellt zu werden. Und das nicht nur, weil sie über solide Portfolios verfügen, sondern weil sie beeindruckende, sichtbare Aufträge erhalten haben – von der beneidenswerten Art, die sich auf unsere visuelle Kultur auswirkt.

Ebenfalls sehr inspirierend ist die große Bandbreite grafischer und konzeptueller Bemühungen aus so vielen Teilen der Welt. Gewisse Stile dominieren hier – Neo-Artnouveau und Neo-déco haben in den vergangenen drei Jahren als ästhetische Reaktion auf die *Art brut*, die sich im vorigen Jahrzehnt durchgesetzt hatte, einen eigenartigen Aufstieg erlebt. Die hochnäsig daherkommende Wiederbelebung der ornamentalen Grafik, insbesondere die sich windenden Ranken und Kletterpflanzen, die auf allem Möglichen von T-Shirts bis zu Buchumschlägen prangt, ist wohl jener Software geschuldet, die die präzise Darstellung und das fehlerlose Wiederholen von Motiven so vereinfacht. Oder es hat vielleicht etwas mit dem nach mehr als einem Jahrzehnt primitiver Formgestaltung steigenden Bedarf an mustergültiger handwerklicher Kunstfertigkeit zu tun. Obwohl skizzenhafte Illustrationen immer noch sehr beliebt sind, wird der Großteil der heutigen Arbeiten von einem leichtherzigen, fröhlichen Unterton begleitet.

Neben stilistischen Trends variieren die Ansätze in der Konzeption stark und auch auf sehr ansprechende Weise. In dieser Ausgabe wird es trotz der amerikanischen Präsidentenwahl des Jahres 2008 wohl weniger eindeutig politische Kommentare geben, aber wir finden eine Fülle von visuellen Anspielungen und anderen, zum Nachdenken anregenden Ideogrammen sowie von weiteren bildlichen Darstellungen, die das Gehirn auf Trab bringen. Und: Die Karikatur – noch vor einem Jahrzehnt als bedroht, wenn nicht gar vollständig komatös betrachtet – kehrt sowohl als Kommentar als auch zur Unterhaltung zurück.

Doch trotz all der beeindruckenden und hervorstechenden Illustrationen, die für diese Ausgabe zusammengestellt wurden, fehlt uns doch etwas: dass etwas wie eine Bombe einschlägt! Damit sind die unvergleichlichen Arbeiten von Einzelnen oder Gruppen gemeint, die auf einem Stil oder Konzept beruhen, das dermaßen treffend den Zeitgeist einfängt (wenn nicht gar prägt), dass sie für immer mit der Zeit verknüpft sein werden, in der sie geschaffen wurden. Doch vielleicht ist es noch zu früh, das zu beurteilen. Ein gewisser Abstand ist immer sehr hilfreich, wenn man etwas beurteilen will, das den Begriff *Zeitgeist* im Namen trägt. Oder vielleicht sind wir ja auch schon über ein solches Phänomen hinaus. So gesund die Illustrationsbranche auch sein mag (und meiner Ansicht ist sie das): Sie ist doch nicht die bedeutsamste der Künste. Die Tage, als James Montgomery Flagg oder Norman Rockwell die populäre Kultur regierten, sind vorbei. Vielleicht ist die Illustration nun (heute) die Summe ihrer Teile. Sollte das der Fall sein, dann schlägt *Illustration Now! Volume 3* vielleicht nicht wie eine Bombe ein, sondern wirkt eher wie eine Streubombe.

Viable et enviable

par Steven Heller

Que nous en soyons au troisième volume de *Illustration Now!* ne devrait pas me surprendre à ce point, mais, honnêtement, je n'ai même jamais imaginé qu'il puisse y en avoir un second, d'autant que lorsque nous avons envisagé de publier le premier, il était permis de douter que les illustrateurs aient un avenir, viable simplement, pas même enviable. De mon point de vue d'éditeur d'art, j'étais convaincu que la demande d'illustration à plat allait céder devant la contraction du marché de la presse écrite, la dépendance grandissante de la photographie, le contrôle à outrance exercé sur l'art et l'abus des exaspérants collages Photoshop. La publicité n'était plus un marché fertile et le royaume de l'édition abordait une période de sècheresse qui promettait d'avoir des effets dévastateurs.

Mais au risque de ressembler à Polyanna (une certaine réserve me paraît préférable), je dois admettre que les choses ont changé – en mieux dans bien des cas. Le puits éditorial n'est plus asséché, et même la publicité commence à reprendre du poil de la bête. Mieux encore, d'autres riches marchés et médias – du jouet à la mode, de l'animation aux jeux vidéo – s'ouvrent à l'illustration, ou à quelque chose qui y ressemble (bien que la ligne entre commerce et beaux arts soit très floue pour certains). Parallèlement à ces raisons d'être optimiste, la crainte omniprésente de voir l'ordinateur tuer l'illustration telle que nous la connaissons et l'aimons s'est révélée infondée –en fait, l'informatique a sans aucun doute rendu l'illustration plus séduisante à bien des égards.

Certes, plusieurs vétérans ont abandonné le champ de bataille pour les chants de sirène des galeries d'art, et d'autres ont été remplacés par une nouvelle vague de jeunes loups, mais il reste encore –et les volumes I, II et III le prouvent– un joli nombre d'illustrateurs extrêmement talentueux et motivés, prêts, résolus et capables de reprendre le flambeau (on dirait un discours de motivation, non ?) et d'inventer des produits novateurs. Pas plus tard qu'aujourd'hui, j'ai rencontré un jeune illustrateur doué d'une telle énergie personnelle et d'un talent brut si impressionnant que j'ai immédiatement eu envie de lui donner quelque chose à faire. Il y a trois ans, j'aurais été bien embarrassé de lui dire où présenter son travail ; aujourd'hui, je peux débiter une douzaine d'endroits où le vendre. Je suis convaincu qu'il a de l'avenir.

Chaque fois que je prononce le mot «marché» un frisson me parcourt l'échine. J'en déteste autant le son que les implications. Très longtemps, j'ai préféré parler de débouchés, et non de marché, pour qualifier les lieux réservés à l'illustration. Pourquoi souiller la profession avec cette vulgaire terminologie commerciale ? Les illustrateurs sont des artistes, n'est-ce pas ? De même que, par extension, les directeurs artistiques qui les commanditent (et les guident). En art, il est admis de créer pour un public réduit à une seule personne. Il est admis que l'artiste refuse d'entendre quand on lui suggère de modifier une œuvre parce qu'elle serait «inappropriée ». On ne doute pas qu'il aille jusqu'à se laisser couper en deux pour défendre l'intégrité de son art. Mais il est ridicule de ne pas voir l'illustration comme un commerce, de peur que l'illustrateur se retrouve sans travail à cause de l'ignorance. L'illustration est manifestement une marchandise créative et l'illustrateur fournit un service au consommateur. La seule différence entre elle et le tout-venant des produits de consommation tient au fait que les illustrateurs offrent davantage qu'un simple objet fonctionnel : ils procurent de l'intelligence visuelle, de l'esthétique et des idées, et, à ce titre, sont employés pour leur habileté à le faire.

Tandis que je me tourmentais, craignant que l'illustration n'ait atteint sa phase terminale, je ne cessais de me demander: qu'est-ce qui pourrait bien la remplacer pour distraire, informer et, parfaitement, faire rêver les gens ? Risque-elle vraiment de connaître le même sort que les silhouettes découpées ou la broderie au point de croix ? Je ne le pense pas. Trop de choses dépendent de l'illustration dessinée ou peinte pour qu'on la laisse dépérir complètement. Nous voici plongés dans *Illustration Now! Volume 3*, et il y a toujours un grand nombre d'illustrateurs, jeunes et moins jeunes, qui valent la peine d'être présentés, non seulement parce qu'ils possèdent de solides portfolios mais parce qu'ils ont mérité d'impressionnantes commandes de premier plan – du genre, enviable, de celles qui ont un effet sur notre culture visuelle.

Le large éventail d'expériences graphiques et conceptuelles qui sont tentées ici et là dans le monde est également encourageant. Certains styles dominent – le néo Art Nouveau et le néo-déco ont connu un essor singulier ces trois dernières années, comme une sorte de réaction esthétique contre l'art brut, prépondérant au cours de la décennie antérieure. Ce renouveau de la rhétorique ornementale graphique, avec en particulier des pampres et des volutes un peu partout, du T-shirt à la jaquette de livre, doit sans doute beaucoup aux logiciels qui assurent aujourd'hui la précision du rendu et facilitent tant la reproduction impeccable. Ou peut-être cela a-t-il quelque chose à voir avec le besoin grandissant de redonner à l'illustration ses lettres de noblesse après une bonne dizaine d'années de style primitif. Bien que l'illustration sommaire soit encore populaire, d'allègres accents de bande dessinée sous-tendent aujourd'hui la plupart des œuvres.

Avec les tendances stylistiques, les approches conceptuelles varient beaucoup elles aussi, et agréablement. En dépit des élections présidentielles américaine de 2008, il y a peut-être moins de commentaires ouvertement politiques dans ce volume, mais on y trouvera davantage de calembours visuels, d'idéogrammes stimulant pour l'esprit et d'images qui suscitent la réflexion. De plus, la caricature, qu'on avait cru en perte de vitesse, voire en danger d'extinction il y a une dizaine d'années, fait un retour en tant que commentaire et divertissement.

Pourtant, malgré le nombre d'illustrations percutantes rassemblées dans ce volume, il y manque quelque chose : la bombe. Le travail incomparable d'un individu ou d'un groupe, basé sur un style ou un concept, qui saisirait si définitivement, ou même définirait, le *zeitgeist*, l'esprit du temps, qu'il serait à jamais indissociable de l'époque où il a été conçu. Peut-être est-il encore trop tôt pour se prononcer. La distance n'est jamais inutile quand on juge quelque chose qui a trait au climat d'une époque. Ou peut-être sommes-nous déjà au-delà d'un tel phénomène. Aussi saine soit-elle – et je pense qu'elle l'est – l'illustration n'est pas le plus important des arts. Les temps où James Montgomery Flagg ou Norman Rockwell régnait sur la culture populaire sont révolus. Peut-être l'illustration est-elle maintenant (aujourd'hui) la somme de ses parties. Si tel est le cas, il se pourrait qu'*Illustration Now! Volume 3* soit, non une bombe classique, mais une bombe à fragmentation.

« *Chaque fois que je prononce le mot ‹ marché ›*
un frisson me parcourt l'échine.
J'en déteste autant le son que les implications. »

150
ILLUSTRATORS
from A to Z

Adam

1961 born in Paris, France | lives and works in Tours, France
http://adam.ultra-book.com

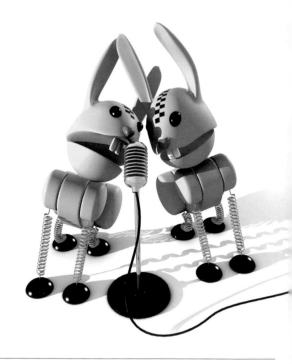

"I carry out a simple and intuitive modelling. I like to adapt the 'retro' style and also to mix the imaginary with reality."

„Ich führe einfache und intuitive Modelle aus. Ich adaptiere gerne eine Art ‚Retro'-Stil und mische frei Erfundenes mit Realem."

« J'exécute une modélisation simple et intuitive. J'aime adapter le style ‹rétro› et mêler l'imaginaire à la réalité. »

↑ *London Series*, 2008, personal work
→ *Velociti*, mascot for Velociti advertising campaign, 2008, Tours
→→ *Edgard*, calendar, 2009, Edgard Opticiens

TOOLS
Blender, Adobe Photoshop

CLIENTS
TBWA Paris, Invacare Europe, American Supply (Sephora), Arch Water Products Europe, Bank Credit Mutuel, Hutchinson

AGENT
Illustrissimo
Paris, France
www.illustrissimo.com

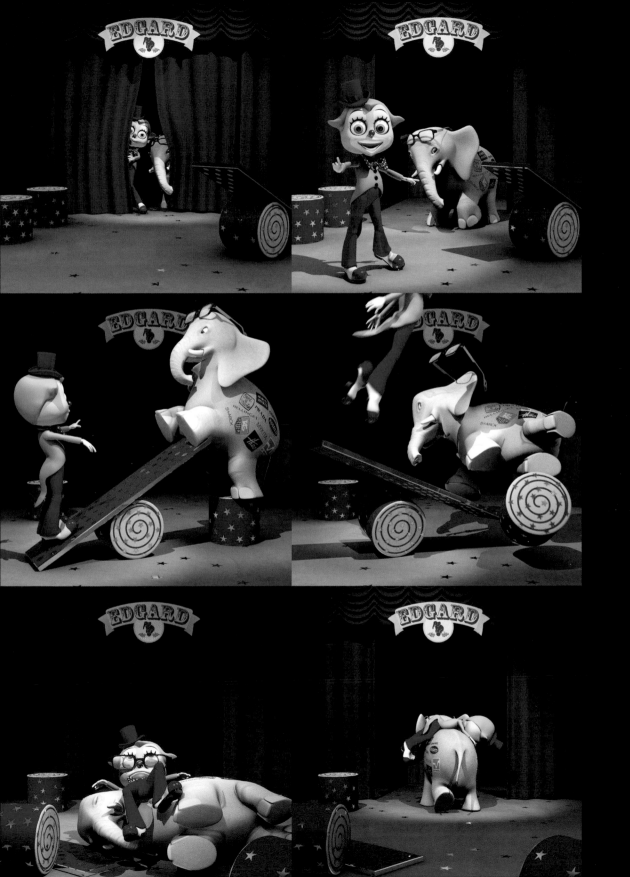

Nik Ainley

1982 born in Oxford, UK | lives and works in Oxford, UK
www.shinybinary.com

"I am constantly trying to further my expertise in digital media, and won't stop until I've mastered the tools I need to realise my ideas fully."

„Ich arbeite beständig daran, besser mit digitalen Medien umgehen zu können, und höre damit erst auf, wenn ich die Tools zur vollständigen Umsetzung meiner Ideen gemeistert habe."

« Je m'efforce constamment de compléter mon expertise en médias numériques, et je n'arrêterai que lorsque je maîtriserai les instruments dont j'ai besoin pour réaliser pleinement mes idées. »

↑   *Type*, 2006, Computer Arts
→   *Oracle*, 2007, personal work
→→ *The Unbearable Lightness of Being*, 2007, personal work

TOOLS
Adobe Photoshop, Adobe Illustrator, Maxon Cinema 4D

CLIENTS
Adobe, MTV, Starbucks, Ericsson, Audi, British Airways, Virgin, National Geographic, HSBC, Faber & Faber, Harper Collins, UNICEF, Esquire, Computer Arts, Digital Arts, Dazed & Confused

SELECTED AWARDS
_Computer Arts Top 10 Up and Coming Creative 2006

SELECTED EXHIBITIONS
_Grand Designs, London, 2007
_Inkthis 2, London, 2007
_ClickforArt, Brick Lane Exhibition
_115 Digital Art Gallery, Bucharest

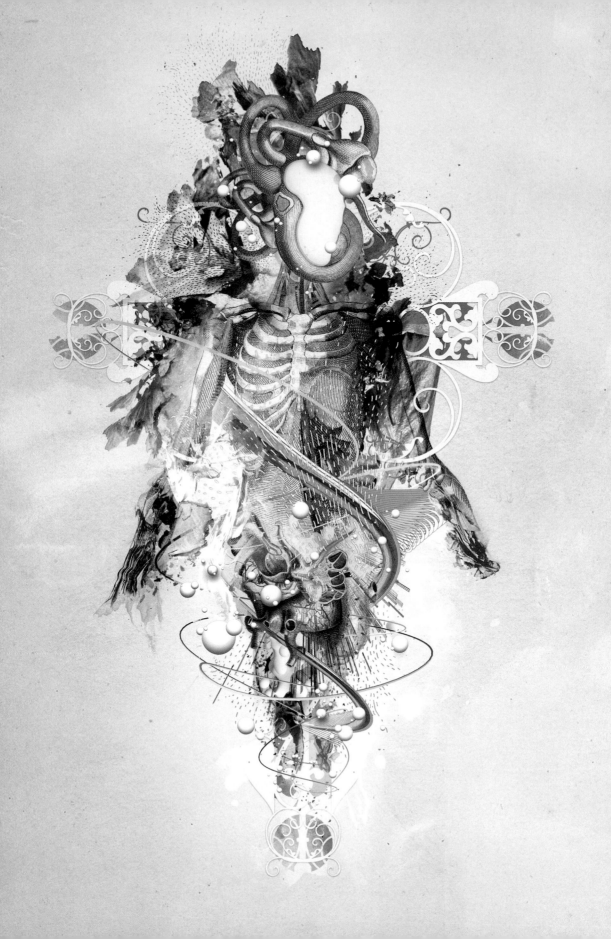

← *Fresh Science Word*, 2008, Computer Arts
→ *Mystic*, 2008, PSDtuts
↓ *Imagine*, 2006, personal work

Douglas Alves

1982 born in São Paulo, Brazil | lives and works in Santa Monica (CA), USA
www.nacionale.net

"Douglas is a dreamer, passionate about nature and surrealist forms."

„Douglas ist ein Träumer und beschäftigt sich leidenschaftlich mit der Natur und surrealistischen Formen.“

« Douglas est un rêveur, passionné par la nature et les formes surréalistes. »

↑   *Mask*, 2008, Color Humano book
→   *Nature Girl Series*, 2008, Hell Group magazine
→→ MTV Brasil, 2007

TOOLS
Adobe Photoshop, Adobe
Illustrator, Wacom tablet

CLIENTS
Microsoft Zune, BBC UK,
MTV Brasil, Citroën Brasil,
Honda Motors, Havaianas,
Burton Snowboards

↑ *Free Bird*, 2008, personal work
→ *Blonde Girl*, 2008, Monarch book
↙ *Torment*, 2008, The Cement
↓ *Djean Sandal*, 2008, DCS Comunicação

Matei Apostolescu

1983 born in Bucharest, Romania | lives and works in Bucharest, Romania
www.013a.com

↑ *From a Much Darker Place*, 2008, personal work
→ *123fourFIVE*, 2006, magazine cover, Computer Arts

"To boldly go where no one has gone before, without moving."

„Kühn dorthin gehen, wohin sich noch nie einer gewagt hat – ohne sich zu bewegen!"

« Aller gaillardement où personne n'est jamais allé, sans faire un mouvement. »

TOOLS
Wacom tablet, Adobe
Photoshop, Adobe Illustrator,
pen, pencil, paper, ink

CLIENTS
Coca-Cola, Olympus, Bombay
Sapphire, Computer Arts UK
& China, Twisted Records,
Otaku magazine

SELECTED AWARDS
_ Design Your Ride
Competition 2006, Runner Up

SELECTED EXHIBITIONS
_ Illustrative, Berlin, 2007
_ 115 Digital Art Gallery,
Bucharest, 2007
_ Ne Placa ce Faci, Bucharest,
2007

↖ *The Waves Extinguish The Wind*, 2007, personal work, exhibited at Illustrative '07 Berlin

→ *Missile Control*, 2009, personal work

← *Everything Beta*, 2008, created for Depthcore no. 33 "Requiem"

Pedro Avella

1975 born in Bogotá, Colombia | lives and works in Cologne, Germany
www.pedroavella.de

↑ *Alter Fritz*, German cookbook, 2008, personal work
→ *Auszogne*, German cookbook, 2008, personal work
→→ *Schneewittchen*, German cookbook, 2008, personal work

"I have lots of fun creating parallel worlds for a specific topic that others can enjoy as well."

„Es macht mir großen Spaß, für ein Thema eine eigene Parallelwelt zu schaffen, an der auch andere sich erfreuen."

« Je prends beaucoup de plaisir à créer des mondes parallèles pour un sujet spécifique que d'autres pourront apprécier à leur tour. »

TOOLS
Acrylic on paper, computer

CLIENTS
Süddeutsche Zeitung, Verlagsgruppe Lübbe, TDK, 24-7medien, 2films, Leyendas, Trias

SELECTED EXHIBITIONS
_ The Köln Concept, Cologne, 2009

Andrew Bannecker

1978 born in Wichita (KS), USA | lives and works in Chicago (IL), New York (NY), and Washington (DC), USA
www.andrewbannecker.com

> *"I dream of digital ink on antique paper. Layering texture upon texture and telling a story."*

> *„Ich träume von digitaler Tinte auf antikem Papier: Texturen übereinander schichten und damit Geschichten erzählen!"*

> *« Je rêve d'encre numérique sur du papier ancien : couche de texture après couche de texture, raconter une histoire. »*

← *Tears of Hope*, 2008, personal work
→ *Uncertainty*, 2007, personal work

TOOLS
Adobe Illustrator, Wacom tablet, vintage ephemera

CLIENTS
Starbucks, Target, Flexjet, Vodafone, Boston Globe, Wallpaper, LA Times, Kashi, Chicago Tribune, Real Simple, Travel and Leisure, Random House, Sainsbury's, Harper Collins, Simon & Schuster

SELECTED AWARDS
_ American Illustration
_ Communication Arts magazine
_ Society of Illustrators
_ Society of Illustrators Los Angeles
_ 3x3 magazine

SELECTED EXHIBITIONS
_ Manifest Hope, Washington DC, USA
_ Monsters Inked

AGENT
Bernstein & Andriulli New York, USA
www.ba-reps.com

Central Illustration London, UK
www.centralillustration.com

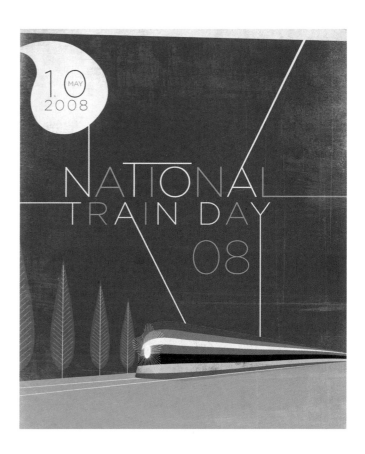

←   *No Turning Back*, 2008, personal work
→   *National Train Day*, 2008, personal work
↓   *Up in Smoke*, 2008, personal work

Justin Bartlett

1977 born in San Diego (CA), USA | lives and works in San Diego (CA), USA, and Oslo, Norway
www.vberkvlt.com

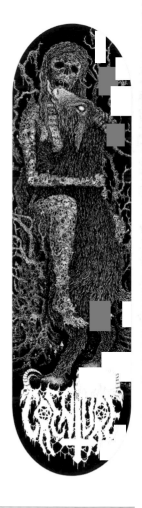

↑ *Chthonic Rites*, gatefold LP illustration and poster, 2007, Moss
→ *Rites of the Goat's Sabbath*, skateboard deck illustration, 2008, Creature Skateboards
→→ *Under the Sign of the Black Mark*, 2009, personal work

"Inspired by religious and theological conflicts, environmental decay, and man's inhumanity – embrace visual hell!!!"

„Inspiration durch religiöse und theologische Konflikte, den Zerfall der Umwelt und die Unmenschlichkeit des Menschen – tauche ein ins Herz der visuellen Hölle!!!"

« Inspiré par les conflits religieux et théologiques, le déclin de l'environnement et l'inhumanité de l'homme – embrasser l'enfer visuel !!! »

TOOLS
Hand-drawn work (micron pens and bristol board), digital, found imagery

CLIENTS
Creature Skateboards, Anti Sweden Jeans, NO Design, Vice magazine, Adbusters Norway, Terrorizer magazine, Apoptygma Berzerk, Aura Noir, Southern Lord Records

SELECTED EXHIBITIONS
_Catalyst, Upper Playground (collective show with Aaron Horkey, Joshua Graham, Seldon Hunt, among others)
_Creatures of the Night exhibition, Supersonic Festival

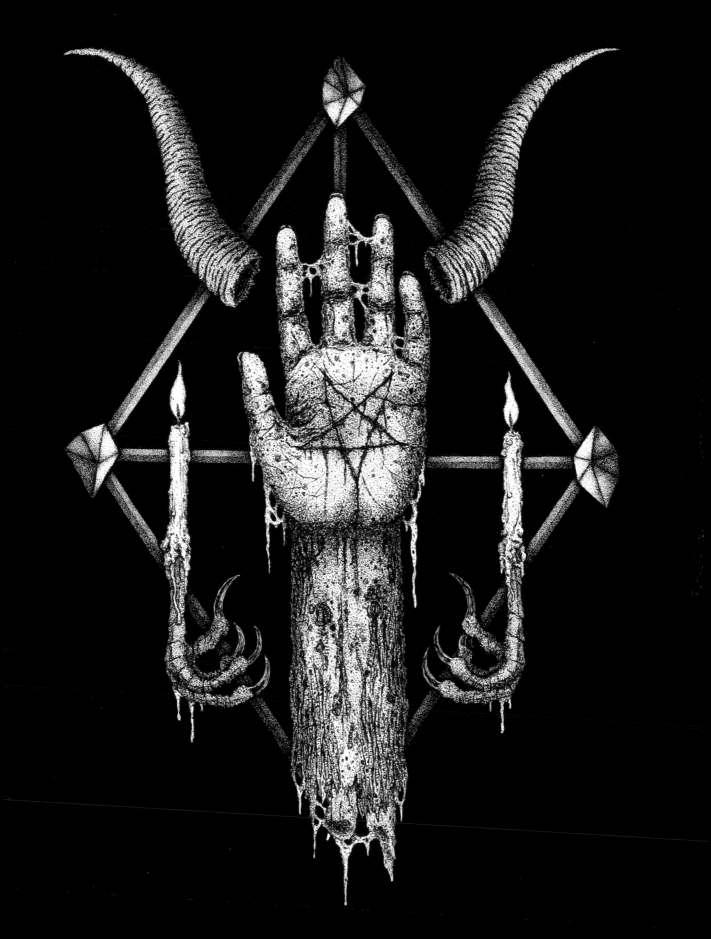

↑   *World Demise*, magazine and poster illustration, 2007,
    Adbusters Norway. Art Director: Halvor Bodin
↓   *Die by the Sword*, 2007, personal work

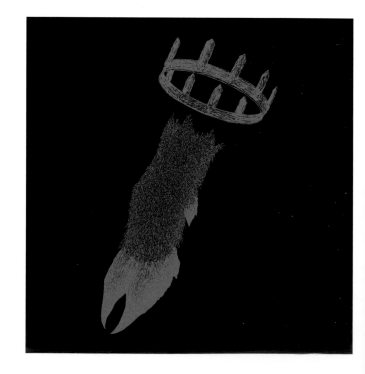

↑   *Dead Raven Choir*, 2008, Oaken Throne magazine
←   *Pazuzu*, CD and LP cover, 2008, Pentemple. Art Director: Stephen O'Malley

Laurent Bazart

1976 born in Nancy, France | lives and works in Malzéville, France
www.supermaxibazar.com

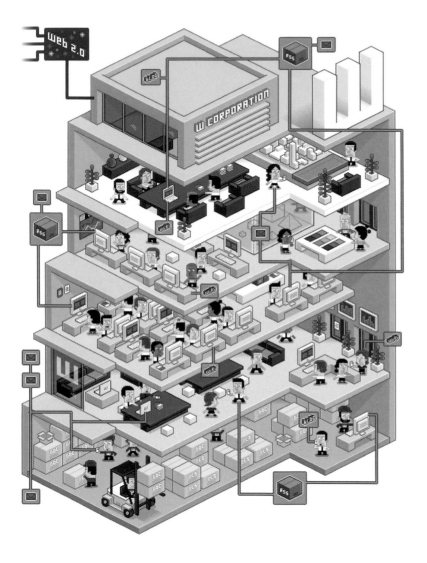

"Assembling pixel elements is about using lo-fi squares in order to create the optical illusion that the depicted images appear in new dimensions."

„Bei der Zusammenstellung von Pixelelementen geht es um die Nutzung einfacher Quadrate, um die optische Illusion zu schaffen, dass die dargestellten Bilder in neuen Dimensionen erscheinen."

« Assembler les éléments pixellisés revient à utiliser des ‹ lo-fi squares › pour donner l'illusion d'optique que les images dépeintes s'affichent dans de nouvelles dimensions. »

↑   *Les Echos*, newspaper article, 2008, Les Echos
→   *Les Inrockuptibles #642*, newspaper article, 2008, Les Inrockuptibles
→→ *VFE magazine #11*, magazine article, 2008, SNCF/VFE, L'Agence Ligaris, Paris

---

TOOLS
Adobe Photoshop, Microsoft Wheel Mouse Optical

CLIENTS
Les Inrockuptibles, Les Echos, Le Monde, SVM Mac, Dada, Bayard, Le Mort-Qui-Trompe, Le Potager Moderne, Microsoft France, SNCF, Textuel, Université de Cergy-Pontoise, Afriquia, Euro RSCG

SELECTED EXHIBITIONS
_ Pixel Contre-Attaque!, Beauvais, France, 2006
_ Le Pixel Art (TV Show "Tracks", ARTE), 2007
_ Blip Festival NYC, 2008

AGENT
Illustrissimo
Paris, France
www.illustrissimo.com

Drew Beckmeyer

1982 born in Los Angeles (CA), USA | lives and works in Los Angeles (CA), USA
www.drewbeckmeyer.com

"My illustration work is done with the intention of being narrative, experimental, and unrepetitive."

„Bei meinen Illustrationen will ich erzählend und experimentell arbeiten und mich nicht wiederholen."

« Mon travail d'illustration se veut narratif, expérimental et non répétitif. »

↑   *I Was Nothing Good, But Now I'm Everything*, 2008, personal work
→   *Fred on Ladder Fort*, 2008, personal work
→→ *I'm Starting to Forget Just How You Look #1*, 2008, personal work

TOOLS
Acrylic, gouache, spray paint, pencils, collage, paper

CLIENTS
The New York Times, ESPN magazine, Howard Hughes Medical Institute, The New York Sun, Esquire Russia, Tiny Showcase, Nuvo magazine

SELECTED EXHIBITIONS
_ Real Deep Thoughts, Tinlark Gallery, Los Angeles, 2008
_ Failure, The LAB/Denver Art Museum, Denver, 2008
_ White Noise, Space 1026, Philadelphia, 2008
_ Parallels of Obstruction, Junc Gallery, Los Angeles, 2007
_ Youngblood, Billy Shire Fine Arts, Culver City, 2006

↑　*Yelling Things That Weren't So Good*, 2008, personal work
←　*Waterslide*, 2008, personal work
→→　*Idea for Economical Man-shower*, 2008, personal work

Eduardo Bertone

1977 born in Rosario, Argentina | lives and works in Madrid, Spain
www.bertoneeduardo.com

← *Freak*, 2008, self-promotion
   for Anna Goodson Managment
→ *Elit*, 2008, LOOKdeBOOK
   magazine & Elit, Stolichnaya vodka

"Different media get fused together in spontaneous, chaotic, and strident ways to wake us up from a sedative and superficial world. Textures and colours enwrap us, representing the visual saturation commonly used to achieve dazzle, and creating dreams, desires, and insecurity."

„Unterschiedliche Medien verschmelzen auf spontane, chaotische und schrille Weise miteinander und wecken uns aus einer betäubenden und oberflächlichen Welt auf. Texturen und Farben umgeben uns. Sie stehen für jene visuelle Sättigung, die häufig als Blendwerk eingesetzt wird und Träume, Begehrlichkeiten und Unsicherheit schafft."

« Différents médias fusionnent de manière spontanée, chaotique et discordante, pour nous réveiller de ce monde anesthésiant et superficiel. Textures et couleurs nous enveloppent, représentant la saturation visuelle communément employée pour éblouir, et provoquant ainsi rêves, désirs et un sentiment d'insécurité. »

TOOLS
Pens, pencils, acrylic, spray paint, watercolour, canvas, wood, paper, recycled materials, Adobe Photoshop

CLIENTS
Leo Burnett Singapore, Boost Mobile L.A., Sixfeet Clothes, Stolichnaya vodka, The Music Awards in Spain, Struendo Filmmakers, Rojo magazine, Smart, Freshcotton Clothes

SELECTED EXHIBITIONS
_Colors Notebook (travelling exhibition), Centre Pompidou/ Triennale di Milano/Shanghai ArtMuseum/Tokyo
_Outsiders Exhibition, Breda, Netherlands
_We Love Sneakers (travelling exhibition), Portugal/Spain

_Rojo Smart Exhibition (travelling exhibition), Invaliden1 Gallery, Berlin/KBB Gallery, Barcelona
_Los Buenos Muñecos Viven Para Siempre, Miscelänea Gallery, Barcelona

AGENT
Anna Goodson Management
Montreal, Canada
www.agoodson.com

Blanquet

1973 born in Conflans St. Honorine, France | lives and works in Paris, France
www.blanquet.com

← *Sweet Teddy*, short story published in Blab! magazine, 2006, Fantagraphics Books
→ *L'Infirmière*, magazine back cover, 2006, Hotwire
↓ *Poupée Mécanique*, 2005, personal work

"I fell into a deep and squalid well in which I drowned; since that day, I have had to wring myself out on paper."

„Ich bin in einen tiefen und schmutzigen Brunnen gefallen und ertrunken. Seit jenem Tag muss ich mich auf dem Papier regelrecht auswringen."

« Je suis tombé dans un puits profond et dégueulasse dans lequel je me suis noyé, depuis ce jour, je dois m'essorer sur le papier. »

TOOLS
Pencil, ink, silkscreen, acrylic painting

CLIENTS
Canal +, Théâtre National de Caen, Arts Factory, Rencontres du 9ème Art, Fantagraphics, Libération

SELECTED EXHIBITIONS
_Festival Périscopages, Rennes, France, 2002
_Labyrinthique Intestin, Chapelle des Pénitents, Aix en Provence, France, 2006
_Blanquet S'ouvre la Panse, Espace Beaurepaire, Paris, 2007
_Cult Fiction (touring exhibition), UK, 2007
_Quintet, Contemporary Art Museum, Lyon, 2009

AGENT
La Superette
Paris, France
www.lasuperette.com

↑　*Aquatic Life*, magazine cover, 2006, Voxer
→　*La Chasse*, CD cover, 2007, Non Stop
←　*La Chienne*, magazine illustration, 2006,
　　Sortez La Chienne Comics

R.O. Blechman

1930 born in Brooklyn (NY), USA | lives and works in Ancram (NY), and New York (NY), USA
www.roblechman.com

↑   *World Trade Center Memorial Lights*, poster, 2007, Municipal Arts Center, New York
→   *Museum Mile*, poster, 1981, Museum Mile Association
→→ *Overpopulation*, magazine cover, 1985, The Atlantic Monthly

"I love doing art in all its forms and guises, but my preferred medium is animation."

„Ich liebe es, in allen möglichen Formen und Gestalten künstlerisch tätig zu sein, doch mein Lieblingsmedium ist die Animation."

« J'adore pratiquer l'art sous toutes ses formes et expressions, mais mon support préféré reste l'animation. »

TOOLS
Pen, watercolour, gouache, Adobe Photoshop

CLIENTS
The New Yorker, IBM, AT&T, PBS, The New York Times, J.P. Morgan Chase Bank, MTV, Perrier, Sony, Procter & Gamble

SELECTED AWARDS
_ Illustrator of the Year AdWeek 1983
_ Art Directors Hall of Fame 1994
_ Cannes Film Festival 1997
_ Biennial Caricature Award 2008

SELECTED EXHIBITIONS
_ Galerie Delpire, Paris, 1968
_ The Graham Gallery, New York, 1978
_ Galerie Bartsch & Chariau, Munich, 1982/1992/1998
_ The Museum of Modern Art, New York, 2003
_ The New York Times Gallery, 2007

AGENT
Reactor Design
Toronto, Canada
www.reactor.ca

Margarethe Hubauer
Hamburg, Germany
www.margarethe-hubauer.com

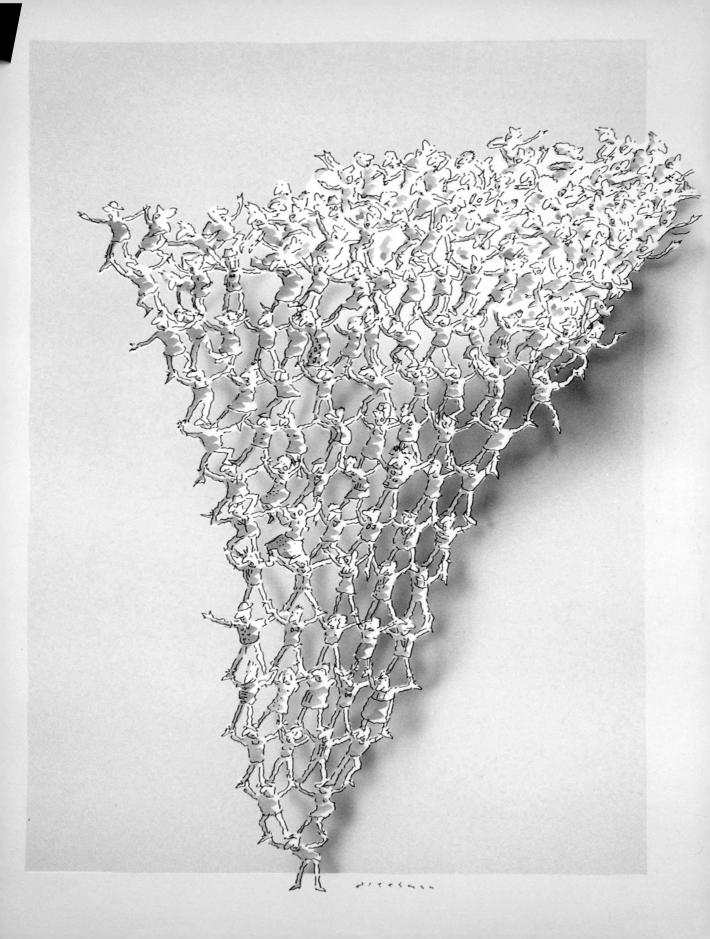

Cathie Bleck

1956 born in Waukegan (IL), USA | lives and works in Cleveland (OH), New York (NY), and Chicago (IL), USA
www.cathiebleck.com

↑ *Mother Nature's Son Two*, "Open Spaces" artist monograph book cover, 2006
→ *Aqua Regia I*, catalog and exhibition "Becoming Human", 2008, Butler Institute of American Art

"I record and observe nature's sensory detail in inks and clay in a medium which has an affinity with wood engraving, illustrating opposing forces."

„Ich beobachte die sinnlichen Details der Natur und halte sie mit Tusche und Ton in einem Medium fest, das dem Holzschnitt gleicht und widerstreitende Kräfte veranschaulicht."

« J'observe et j'enregistre les détails sensoriels de la nature à l'aide d'encres et de glaise, sur un support qui n'est pas sans rappeler la gravure sur bois, illustrant ainsi des forces contraires. »

TOOLS
Clay board, scratchboard, ink, kaolin clay, razors

CLIENTS
The New York Times, Simon & Schuster, FSG, Knopf, Harper, Martha Stewart Living, Fast, Esquire, Sony, U.S. Postal Service, Time magazine, The Wall Street Journal, Warner Bros., Random House

SELECTED AWARDS
_ Museum of American Illustration
_ Spectrum Annuals
_ American Illustration Annuals
_ Society of Illustrators
_ Communication Arts magazine

SELECTED EXHIBITIONS
_ The Butler Institute of American Art, solo exhibition, 2008
_ New Britain Museum of American Art, mid-career retrospective, 2008
_ Open Spaces, I Space Gallery, University of Illinois, 2006
_ Norman Rockwell Contemporary Woman Illustrators, 2004
_ 43 Woman Artists from Around the World, Associazione Culturale Teatrio, 2006–2007 (Exhibition tour in Italy)

↑   *Mother Nature's Son Three*, "Open Spaces"
    artist monograph book cover, 2006
→   *Rethinking Deforestation*, 2006,
    The New York Times
→→ *Nature's Myth*, poster, 2007,
    commissioned by the U.S. State Department,
    for the 2007 U.S. Earth Day

Paul Blow

1969 born in Falkirk, UK | lives and works in Dorset, UK
www.paulblow.com

← *Oil*, 2008, The Guardian
→ *Love Bites*, 2008, Independent magazine
↓ *Police*, 2008, Radio Times, UK

*"Much of the commissioned work is editorial, and
I find creating complex, compelling imagery within
a narrative context to be immensely rewarding."*

„*Ein Großteil meiner Auftragsarbeit ist redaktionell. Ich empfinde
es als unglaublich bereichernde Aufgabe, komplexe und fesselnde bildliche
Darstellungen in einem narrativen Kontext schaffen zu dürfen.*"

« *Une grande partie du travail de commande provenant de l'édition,
créer des images complexes et séduisantes dans un contexte
narratif me semble extrêmement gratifiant.* »

TOOLS
Mixed media

CLIENTS
The Guardian, Independent
magazine, The FT, Time
magazine, New Scientist,
Reader's Digest, BBC, LA
magazine, New York magazine,
Harvard Business Review,
Stanford Medicine, Design
Week, Saatchi & Saatchi

SELECTED AWARDS
_ Association of Illustrators
(Best of British Illustration)
_ 3x3 magazine
_ V&A Illustration Awards
2007
_ Transport for London Silver
Award

SELECTED EXHIBITIONS
_ Paul Blow (Forty), 2009
_ Paul Blow (Narratives and
Nausea), 2008

AGENT
Anna Goodson Management
Montreal, Canada
www.agoodson.com

Eastwing
London, UK
www.eastwing.co.uk

→   *Schools Out!*, 2008, Independent magazine
↘   *Speech*, 2008, The Guardian

↑   *To Kill a Mockingbird*, 2008, self-promotion
→   *Secret*, 2009, Readers Digest, Canada

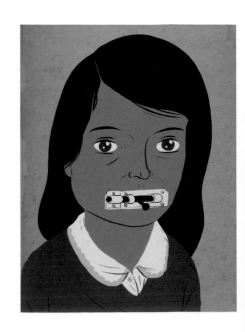

Darren Booth

1978 born in Sault Ste. Marie, Ontario, Canada | lives and works in St. Catharines, Ontario, Canada
www.darrenbooth.com

"I try to keep my artistic influences at a distance in order to try to find my own voice and try to find inspiration from non-artistic places."

„Ich versuche, mich von künstlerischen Beeinflussungen frei zu halten, um meine eigene Stimme zu finden und mich an ‚un-künstlerischen' Orten inspirieren zu lassen."

« J'essaie de garder à distance mes influences artistiques afin de trouver ma propre voix, en tâchant de tirer l'inspiration d'endroits qui n'ont rien à voir avec l'art. »

↑　*Think Green*, magazine cover, 2007, The Chicago Tribune magazine
　　Art Director: Joe Darrow
→　*Work Life*, book cover, 2008, Uppercase Gallery/Vangool Design
→→ *Jimi Hendrix*, 2008, personal work

TOOLS
Acrylic, collage on treated paper

CLIENTS
Coca-Cola, Target, ESPN, BBDO, The New York Times, The Los Angeles Times, Penguin Books, Canada Post Corporation, Billboard magazine

SELECTED AWARDS
_American Illustration
_The Society of Illustrators, New York
_The Society of Illustrators, Los Angeles
_The Type Directors Club
_Communication Arts

SELECTED EXHIBITIONS
_Heaven and Hell Exhibition, Murphy Design
_The Art of Burlesque
_The Society of Illustrators, New York
_Old School, Uppercase Gallery
_Work/Life, Uppercase Gallery

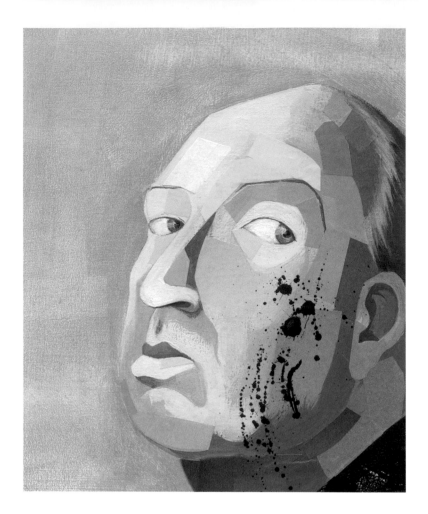

↑   *Hitchcock*, 2007, personal work
→   *Halo*, 2006, personal work

↑ *Bridge to Nowhere*, 2006, The New York Times
   magazine. Art Director: Gail Bichler
→ *Platypus*, *Armadillo*, wine labels, 2007, Vincor
↓ *Bobcat*, wine label, 2007, Vincor

Syd Brak

1936 born in Johannesburg, South Africa | lives and works in London, UK
www.sydbrak.co.uk

↑　*Trident Lady*, press advertising, 2008, JWT
→　*Sexy Beast*, film poster, 2000
→→ *Robbie Robot*, film poster

"I have always thought of myself as an illustrator as opposed to an artist. Although both require the same talents the motivations are different. An artist paints for himself. An illustrator paints for others."

„Ich habe mich immer weniger als Künstler und mehr als Illustrator empfunden. Obwohl beide die gleichen Talente brauchen, unterscheidet sich deren Motivation doch: Ein Künstler malt für sich selbst, ein Illustrator für andere."

« Je me suis toujours perçu comme un illustrateur, non comme un artiste. Les mêmes talents sont nécessaires dans les deux cas, mais les motivations different. L'artiste peint pour lui-même. L'illustrateur pour les autres. »

TOOLS
Airbrush, watercolour, Adobe Photoshop, pencil, crayon

CLIENTS
Coca-Cola, Guinness, Pepsi, Gordon's Gin, Jim Bean, Natwest, Royal Mail, Cadbury's, Mars, Walls Dolmio, The Guardian, PlayStation, Trident

SELECTED AWARDS
_Creative Circle Award

SELECTED EXHIBITIONS
_Travelling Exhibition, various advertising agencies, 2006–2009

Steve Brodner

1954 born in Brooklyn (NY), USA | lives and works in New York (NY), USA
www.stevebrodner.com

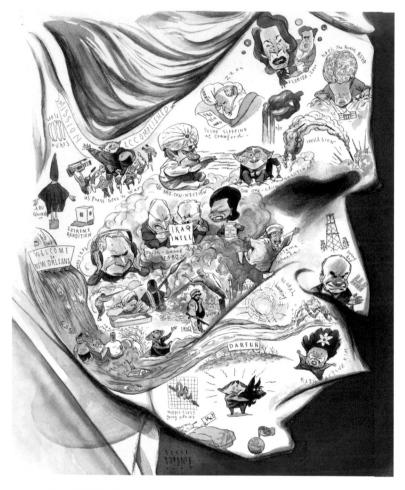

"Illustration is about storytelling. If done well it is compelling, beautiful, and unforgettable."

„Bei Illustrationen geht's ums Geschichtenerzählen. Wird das gut gemacht, ist es überzeugend, wunderschön und unvergesslich."

« Illustrer, c'est raconter des histoires. Si c'est bien fait, c'est irrésistible, beau et inoubliable. »

↑   *Bush Profile*, 2007, Texas Monthly
→   *Bush Victory Cigar*, 2004, Rolling Stone
→→ *Red, New York, and Blue*, page two of Election Cartoon, 2008, The New Yorker

---

TOOLS
Paper, watercolour

CLIENTS
The New Yorker, The Nation, Rolling Stone, The Atlantic, Mother Jones

SELECTED AWARDS
_ Aronson Award for Social Justice Journalism
_ Hamilton King Award (Society of Illustrators)
_ Reuben Award (Art magazine NCS)
_ Society of Illustrators
_ Art Directors Club

SELECTED EXHIBITIONS
_ Career Retrospective, Norman Rockwell Museum, 2008
_ Society of Illustrators Annual Show

RED and BLUE NEW YORK.

A POLITICAL junkie re-emerges on Election DAY to DISCOVER that NOW NOTHING is the SAME...

by STEVE BRODNER

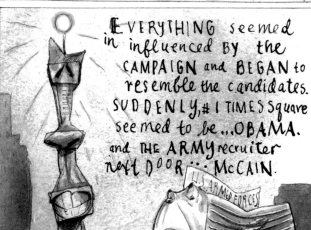

EVERYTHING seemed in influenced BY the CAMPAIGN and BEGAN to resemble the candidates. SUDDENLY, #1 TIMES Square seemed to be...OBAMA. and THE ARMY recruiter next DOOR... McCAIN.

U.S. ARMED FORCES

Pedicabs...McCAIN

Strollers... OBAMA

↑   *Steve Jobs/Beatles*, 2007, Fortune magazine
←   *Hillary et al*, 2008, Newsweek
←← *Presidents of the United States*, 2009, Mother Jones

Brosmind

2006 founded in Barcelona, Spain | is Alejandro Mingarro & Juan Mingarro
www.brosmind.com

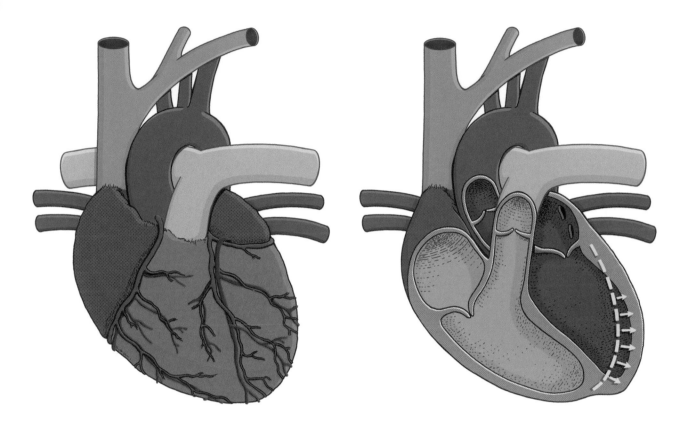

↑   *Heart*, medical book "Corazón y Mente" by Valentín Fuster
    and Luis Rojas Marcos, 2008, Planeta
→   *Sir Pantry*, from the project "What's Inside" by Brosmind, 2009

"Our work is optimistic and always combines fantasy and humour."

„Unsere Arbeit ist optimistisch und verbindet stets Fantasie und Humor."

« Notre travail est optimiste et il allie toujours fantaisie et humour. »

TOOLS
Pencil, ink, paper, computer

CLIENTS
Honda, 55DSL, Pepsi,
Excedrin, Etapes magazine

SELECTED AWARDS
_ Cannes Lions 2007
_ Laus Trophy 2007
_ Sol de Oro San Sebastian
2008
_ Shortlist Cannes Lions 2008

SELECTED EXHIBITIONS
_ Art&Clash, Zurich
_ Offjectes, Barcelona
_ Conversational Spanish,
Aram Gallery, London
_ Spain Again, Tokyo
_ Uniqform, Basel

AGENT
Levine/Leavitt
New York, USA
www.llreps.com

↑   *Diploma*, real size championship belt for school degree, 2008,
    Elisava Design school, Barcelona
←   *Meatman*, cover of the magazine "ETAPES diseño y cultura" #4,
    2008, ETAPES Graphic Design magazine
→   *Money*, and *Beauty*, press advertising, 2008, Excedrin
    Agency: Saatchi & Saatchi, New York
↓   *El Caganer*, chocolate package, 2008, Enric Rovira
    Photographer: Meritxel Arjalaguer

Daniel Bueno

1974 born in São Paulo, Brazil | lives and works in São Paulo, Brazil
www.buenozine.com.br

↑ *Caçador Espacial*, "Nove Chapeuzinhos" children's book by Flavio de Souza, 2007, Companhia das Letras
→ *Histórias de Bicho Feio*, book cover, 2008, Companhia das Letras

*"I work with geometric shapes and collage, using graphic elements as entities
that can have another meaning. There's abstraction, illusion, fantasy."*

*„Ich arbeite mit geometrischen Formen und Collagen, wobei ich grafische Elemente als eigenständige Einheiten einsetze,
die auch andere Bedeutungen haben können. Da erscheinen Abstraktionen, Illusionen und Fantasien."*

*« Je travaille avec les formes géométriques et le collage, en utilisant les éléments graphiques comme autant de concepts
susceptibles d'avoir une autre signification. Il y a de l'abstraction, de l'illusion, de la fantaisie. »*

TOOLS
Rough in pencil, manual
collages with paper, cut-out
magazines and newspapers,
acrylics, other materials, Adobe
Photoshop

CLIENTS
Cosac Naify, Companhia
das Letras, Martins Fontes,
Salamandra, Folha de São
Paulo, Editora Abril, Editora
Globo, Livraria Cultura,
Revista da TAM, Trip, Lobo,
Ernst & Young, Unibanco

SELECTED AWARDS
_ Salão Internacional de
Desenho para a Imprensa
de Porto Alegre 2003
_ Prêmio Jabuti 2006
_ Prix Ars Elestronica 2005
_ Prêmio HQ Mix 2007/2008

SELECTED EXHIBITIONS
_ 46th and 47th Annual
Exhibition, Society of
Illustrators, New York,
2004/2005
_ Annecy Festival, Short Films
Panorama, France, 2005
_ Ottawa Festival, Canada, 2005

_ Tercero Encuentro
Internacional de Comix
de La Paz, Bolivia, 2005
_ Football Heroes Expo,
Lucerne, Switzerland, 2006

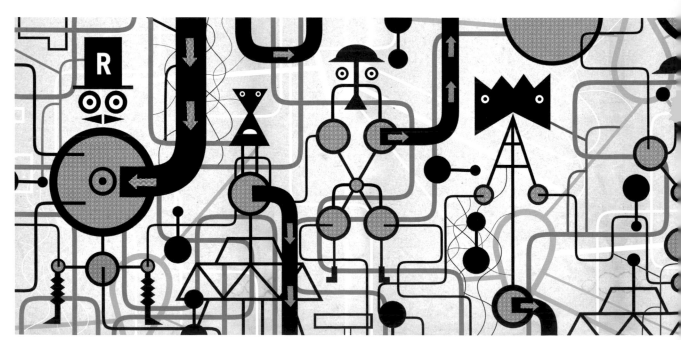

← *Engrenagens*, 2004, Macmania magazine
↗ *MacIntel: They Are Coming*, magazine cover, 2006, Macmania magazine
→ *Untitled*, 2008, personal work
↓ *Fluxos*, 2007, Nueva Sociedad magazine

Mitchy Bwoy

1998 founded in London, UK
http://mitchybwoy.tumblr.com

> *"Always inspire,
> never dictate."*
>
> „Immer inspirieren,
> niemals diktieren."
>
> « Toujours inspirer,
> jamais dicter ses lois. »

↑ *Hurt You*, 2008, Ram Records, Chase & Status
→ *Mpho Skeef*, 2006, Wall of Sound, PIAS
→→ *"Stripes" Clown Girl*, T-shirt, 2008, Addict clothing

TOOLS
Pen, ink, vector and
pixel-based computer
applications

CLIENTS
Addict clothing, Wall of Sound
Records, Ram Records,
Z Records, Bluey Music,
Pantone Music, Future Soul
Records, Defected Records,
Esquire magazine, Chaser
magazine, XLR8R magazine

SELECTED EXHIBITIONS
_ "Miami Vices" group show,
Art Basel, Miami 2002
_ "Loud Graphix Berlin"
group show, Berlin 2007
_ Solo show, Contact Theatre,
Manchester 2007
_ Solo show, Craze Gallery,
London 2008

_ "Hell Hath no Fury" joint
show with Rabodiga, 55DSL
Art Space, London 2008

Dave Calver

1954 born in Rochester (NY), USA | lives and works in Palm Springs (CA), USA
www.davecalver.com

"I hope people see elegance and humor in all of my work. In the gallery work I've been able to push the humor in less expected directions."

„Ich hoffe, dass die Menschen in meiner gesamten Arbeit Eleganz und Humor erkennen. In meinen Arbeiten für Galerien konnte ich den Humor in ganz unerwartete Richtungen vorantreiben.“

« J'espère que les gens perçoivent de l'élégance et de l'humour dans tout ce que je fais. Dans mon travail de galerie, j'ai réussi à pousser l'humour dans les directions les plus inattendues. »

↑   *Spring*, cover, 2000, American Showcase
→   *The Headless Smoker*, 2004, personal work
→→ *Drunken Mammals*, 2008, personal work

TOOLS
Coloured pencils, acrylic on paper

CLIENTS
American Express, CBS, Comedy Channel, HBO, IBM, Bloomingdale's, Mobil, Vogue, Newsweek, Playboy, Random House, Rolling Stone, Sports Illustrated, Time magazine, United Airlines, Vanity Fair

SELECTED AWARDS
_ Society of Illustrators
_ Communication Arts magazine
_ Society of Publication Designers
_ American Illustration
_ Art Directors Club

SELECTED EXHIBITIONS
_ Moods for Moderns (Brad Benedict's Side Show, Part 2), Robert Bernan Gallery, Los Angeles, 2008
_ Now Brow (Brad Benedict's Side Show, Part 3), Wal-Art, Los Angeles, 2008
_ American Pop Culture Images, La Foret Museum, Tokyo, 1986
_ One Man Show, Little Gallery, Nazareth College, Rochester, 1995
_ One Man Show, Rochester Institute of Technology, 2000

AGENT
Morgan Gaynin Inc.
New York, USA
www.morgangaynin.com

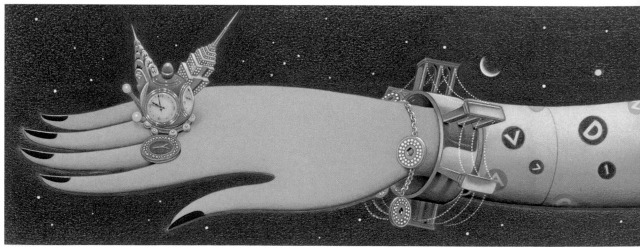

↑ *Doomed Procession*, 2008, Brad Benedict's "Side Show"
at Robert Bernan Gallery, personal work
← *Last Call at the Garnish Bar*, for "Freaky Tiki" Light Gallery, 2008, personal work
→ *Face*, cover art for "Beauty" section, 1994, New Jersey Monthly
↓ *NYC Bling*, 2007, New York City Mass Transit Authority

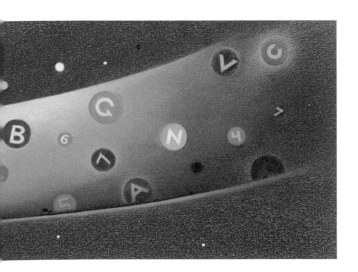

Stephen Campbell

1966 born in Corpus Christi (TX), USA | lives and works in New York (NY), and Birmingham (AL), USA
www.art-dept.com/illustration/campbell

"My work is like paper cut-outs with many layers; humor, details, and color are the most important. My figures have just enough information to do their job."

„Meine Arbeiten sind wie Scherenschnitte mit vielen Schichten; dabei sind Humor, Details und Farben das Wichtigste. Meine Bilder enthalten gerade genug Informationen, um ihre Aufgabe erledigen zu können."

« Mon travail s'apparente à plusieurs couches successives de papier déchiré ; l'humour, les détails et la couleur sont ce qu'il y a de plus important. Mes silhouettes ont juste assez d'information pour faire leur boulot. »

↑   *Girl's Best Friend*, 2008, self-promotion
→   *Converse*, 2008, Vogue Bambini
→→ *Claire*, 2008, self-promotion

TOOLS
Adobe Illustrator, hand-stitched on fabric

CLIENTS
Vogue Bambini, Numéro Beauté, Elle, Travel+Leisure, Bloomingdale's, John Lewis Department Store, Nikon, H&M, Liz Lange Maternity, Dreamworks, Bliss Spa, Dayton Hudson

AGENT
Art Department
New York, USA
www.art-dept.com

Serlin Associates
London, UK
www.serlinassociates.com

Innovative Fashion Ideas
Milan, Italy
www.innovativefashionideas.com

Cecilia Carlstedt

1977 born in Stockholm, Sweden | lives and works in New York (NY), Stockholm, Sweden, and London, UK
www.ceciliacarlstedt.com

> *"I love to experiment with contrasts and textures and strive for the unexpected when I work."*

„Ich liebe es, mit Kontrasten und der Beschaffenheit von Oberflächen zu experimentieren. Bei der Arbeit ziele ich auf Unerwartetes ab."

« J'adore expérimenter les contrastes et les textures ; c'est à l'inattendu que j'aspire dans mon travail. »

↑   *Untitled*, 2006, personal work
→   *Untitled*, portrait of the winner, 2008,
    Council of Fashion Designers of America Awards
→→ *Untitled*, 2006, The Sunday Telegraph

TOOLS
Pencil, ink, screenprinting, Adobe Photoshop, Adobe Illustrator

CLIENTS
H&M, La Perla, Vidal Sassoon, Victoria Beckham, Swarovski, Ricci Ricci, Waterman Pens, LA Times, Vogue (Nippon, UK, and India), Elle, Marie Claire

AGENT
Art Department
New York, USA
www.art-dept.com

The Anna Su Agency
London, UK
www.theannasuagency.com

Agent Bauer
Stockholm, Sweden
www.agentbauer.com

Esther Casas Roura

1977 born in Barcelona, Spain | lives and works in New York (NY), USA
www.claymaniak.com

"I own my observations of the world through my characters, in their own environment, and I allow no limitations on subject matter."

„Durch die Augen meiner Charaktere in ihrer Umgebung eigne ich mir deren Blick auf die Welt an, und ich lasse keine Einschränkungen zu, was die Thematik angeht."

« Je m'approprie ma perception du monde à travers mes personnages, dans leur propre environnement, et je n'admets de limites sur aucun sujet. »

↑   *Sal, the most emblematic pizzeria man in New York*, 2008, personal work
↖   *Piquete, Madre de Mayo y Cacerolera*, 2005, Gaspar Libedinsky
→→ *Louie Vega*, 2006, Louie Vega, Vega Records

TOOLS
Clay, silicone, plastic, wire, rasps, brushes, digital camera, Adobe Photoshop, Adobe After Effects, Final Cut Pro

CLIENTS
Dorian Orange Studio, Reebok Ltd., Louie Vega, Blackerrabit Art&Entertainment Group, The Fresh Element Sound Records

SELECTED EXHIBITIONS
_ Online magazine group exhibition, International Design Network (IdN)
_ Sculpture collective exhibition, The Art Students League, New York

Guillaumit Castagne

1980 born in Martel, France | lives and works in Lormont, France
www.guillaumit.com

↑ *Chorale*, poster, 2009, Gangpol & Mit
→ *Face*, 2008, personal work
→→ *Family*, 2008, personal work

"My work combines geometric forms, rigid colour schemes, and funny cartoon characters."

„In meiner Arbeit kombiniere ich geometrische Formen, strenge Farbschemata und lustige Zeichentrickfiguren."

« Mon travail combine les formes géométriques, les schémas de couleur rigides et de drôles de personnages de dessins animés. »

TOOLS
Adobe Illustrator

CLIENTS
BBmix Festival, Sony France, Leo Burnett, Threadless, Coltesse

SELECTED EXHIBITIONS
_Arts Factory Summer Show, Paris
_Miou's, Tokyo
_Festival de la Creatividad, Florence
_Pictoplasma Berlin, 2008

AGENT
Lezilus
Paris, France
www.lezilus.com

Seounghyon Cho

1976 born in Daejeon, South Korea | lives and works in New York (NY), USA
www.choillustration.com

"Stories are continually unfolding around us. I try to listen carefully and describe the details of the world through my own unique perspective."

„Fortwährend entfalten sich Geschichten um uns herum. Ich versuche, genau zuzuhören, und beschreibe die Details der Welt durch meine eigene, ganz individuelle Perspektive."

« Des tas d'histoires se déroulent sans cesse autour de nous. J'essaie d'être à l'écoute et de rendre les détails du monde à travers ma perspective personnelle. »

↑   *Agoraphobia (fear of open spaces)*, 2008, personal work
→   *Eurotophobia (fear of female genitalia)*, 2008, personal work
→→ *Didaskaleinophobia (fear of going to school)*, 2008, personal work

TOOLS
Encaustic wax

CLIENTS
The Deal magazine, RVA magazine, Hemingway, 3x3 magazine

SELECTED AWARDS
_ American Illustration 2008
_ Creative Quarterly 2008
_ Noma Concours 2008

SELECTED EXHIBITIONS
_ Book Show, Visual Art Gallery, NY, 2007
_ Thesis Show, Visual Art Gallery, NY, 2008
_ The Character, School of Visual Art Gallery, NY, 2008
_ Face time, School of Visual Art Gallery, NY, 2009

← *Aviophobia (fear of flying)*, 2008, personal work
↗ *Shoemaker* , 2008, personal work
→ *At Midnight*, 2009, personal work
↓ *Claustrophobia (fear of confined spaces)*, 2008, personal w

Ief Claessen

1970 born in Neerpelt, Belgium | lives and works in Ghent, and Antwerp, Belgium | also known as Gideon Kiefer
www.flickr.com/photos/iefclaessen

← *The Autodidact*, 2008, personal work
→ *Experiment*, 2009, Het Parool
↓ *Wiedergutmachung*, 2008, personal work

*"When I work, I feel like a director
and his whole film crew in one.
I always try to reinvent myself."*

*„Wenn ich arbeite, fühle ich mich gleichzeitig
wie ein Regisseur und dessen Filmcrew.
Ich versuche immer, mich neu zu erfinden."*

*« Quand je travaille, j'ai l'impression d'être
tout à la fois le cinéaste et l'équipe de tournage.
J'essaie toujours de me réinventer. »*

TOOLS
Pencil, pen, gouache, ink, ecoline, acrylic, coloured pencils, paper, hardboard, Adobe Photoshop, Wacom tablet, digital camera, scans

CLIENTS
De Morgen, De Tijd, Trends, Het Parool, De Groene Amsterdammer, Humo, Knack, Weekend Knack, Klasse, Yeti, Clavis, Vanin

SELECTED AWARDS
_ Young Lions Book Awards 2008 (nomination)
_ Tilly van Eersel Award (nomination)
_ Hedgehog Award (nomination)

SELECTED EXHIBITIONS
_ Modernism, Hove Academy, Antwerp, 2008
_ Decennial Weliswaar, Boudewijn Building, Brussels, 2005
_ Retrospective, Cultural Institute Dommelhof, Neerpelt, 2004

_ Comics, Mekanik Comic Store, Antwerp, 2000
_ Tangoscoop, K.A.S.K.A., Antwerp, 2000

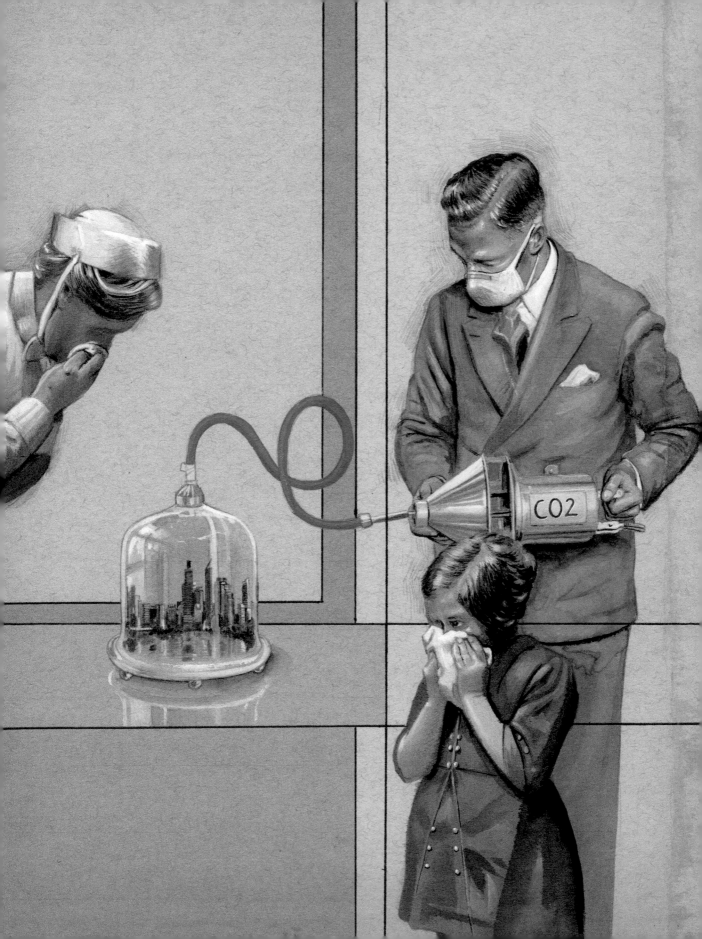

Alejandro Colu--i

1966 born in Montevideo, Uruguay | lives and works in Barcelona, Spain
www.alejandrocolucci.com

"*I'm interested in dark, atmospheric work. I think that my paintings are influenced by comics and illustration work of the '70s and '80s, and also by silent movies.*"

„Mich interessieren besonders dunkle und atmosphärische Arbeiten. Ich finde, dass meine Gemälde von Comics und illustrativen Arbeiten der 70er und 80er Jahre, aber auch von Stummfilmen beeinflusst werden."

« J'aime travailler les atmosphères sombres. Je pense que mes peintures sont influencées par l'illustration et les bandes dessinées des années 70 et 80, mais aussi par le cinéma muet. »

↑ *Journey into the Void*, book cover, 2005, Timun Mas
→ *Desmodus*, notebook cover, 1997, Papiros
→→ *Vampires, A Book of Legends II*, 2007, personal work

TOOLS
Pencil, gouache, oil painting, Adobe Photoshop, Wacom tablet

CLIENTS
Random House Mondadori, Grupo Planeta, Grupo Zeta, Grupo El Mundo, Santillana, Éditions Robert Laffont, Dolmen Books, Alamut Ediciones, Maeva Ediciones, White Wolf Publishing

SELECTED AWARDS
_First National Comic Contest of Argentina 2000

SELECTED EXHIBITIONS
_Comic Museum, Uruguay, 1996
_Buquebus Foundation, Uruguay, 1999

Alexandra Compain-Tissier

1971 born in Paris, France | lives and works in Paris, France
www.alexandracompaintissier.com

"I would define my style as realistic, feminine, and contemporary illustration. I like to create fashion stories, from the concept to the realisation."

„Ich würde meinen Stil als realistische, feminine und zeitgenössische Illustration definieren. Ich liebe es, Fashion-Storys zu schaffen – vom Konzept bis hin zur Realisierung."

« Pour définir mon style, je parlerais d'illustration réaliste, féminine et contemporaine. J'aime créer des ‹fashion stories›, de la conception à la réalisation. »

↑→ *My Favorite Margiela Things*, 2005,
  Maison Martin Margiela, Bon magazine
→→ *Emilie & Dora*, 2006, OFR publication
  Art Director: Sophie Toporkoff

TOOLS
Watercolours on paper, pencil on paper

CLIENTS
Saks Fifth Avenue, Maison Martin Margiela, Diesel, American Express, EMI, Colette, Uniqlo, Harvard University, Sujet Japan, Comet Records, Harbour City Mall Hong Kong, Graniph Japan

SELECTED EXHIBITIONS
_ MY 2007, Boutique Colette, Paris, 2007
_ Solo exhibition, Perif Galerie, Beijing, 2007
_ Traits Très Mode (world traveling exhibition of fashion illustration), 2007
_ Remastered, San Francisco, 2006
_ Christie's, Amesterdam, 2006

AGENT
Art Department
New York, USA
www.art-dept.com

← *Vincent & Gabriel*, promo book, 2009,
Art Department
←← *Belle de Jour*, promo book, 2009,
Art Department
→ *Inaki*, portrait of the French cook
at "Le Chateaubriand, Paris", 2009,
GQ France
→→ *Untitled*, 2007, Esquire magazine Russia

← *Saks Windows*, shopping bags and campaign, 2008,
Saks Fifth Avenue, New York
Creative Director: Terron Schaefer
→ *Make You Imagine*, poster, 2007, Le Coq Sportif Japan
Model: Sophie Toporkoff

James Cooper

1980 born in Sydney, Australia | lives and works in Sydney, Australia, and Dublin, Ireland
www.dreamer-design.com

↑ *Every Man Wants The World*, single cover, 2008, Whitewash Recordings
→ *All I Want Is You*, album graphics, *2007*, Sony Music
→→ *Alice*, 2008, cover art, Desktop magazine

"My work begins as raw, pencil-driven illustration. Colour, line work, and patterns play a large part in my process. To draw is to play."

„Meine Arbeit beginnt als grobe Bleistiftskizze. Farben, Linien und Muster spielen in meiner Arbeitsweise eine große Rolle. Zeichnen ist Spielen."

« Au départ de mon travail, il y a l'illustration brute, au crayon. La couleur, le travail des lignes et les motifs jouent un rôle important dans ma façon de procéder. Dessiner, c'est jouer. »

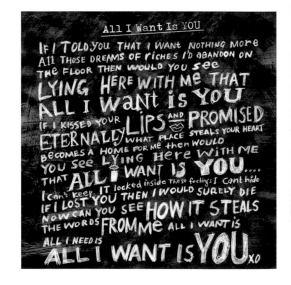

TOOLS

Pencil, brush, ink, marker pen, paint, digital camera, photocopy, Adobe Photoshop

CLIENTS

Sony Music, Harlequin Publishers, Avant Card, Warner Music, Allen & Unwin Publishers

Etienne Delessert

1941 born in Lausanne, Switzerland | lives and works in Lakeville (CT), USA
www.etiennedelessert.com

↑ *Silly Story No.3 by Eugene Ionesco,* "The toys" children's book, 2008, Editions Gallimard Jeunesse
→ *Happy Christmas 2008?,* 2008, Siné Hebdo magazine

"Translating my own and the world's ideas, passions, fantasies, and nightmares into the visual language of books, magazine illustrations, posters, animated films, paintings, and sculptures."

„Ich übersetze eigene Ideen, Leidenschaften, Fantasien und Alpträume und die der Welt in die visuelle Sprache von Büchern, Zeitschriftenillustrationen, Postern, Trickfilmen, Gemälden und Skulpturen.“

« Traduire ma propre conception du monde, mes passions, mes fantasmes et mes cauchemars dans le langage visuel des livres, des illustrations de revues, des affiches, des films d'animation, de la peinture et de la sculpture. »

TOOLS
Watercolour, pencils, acrylics

CLIENTS
New York Times, Le Monde, The New Yorker, Time magazine, The Atlantic , Creative Editions, Gallimard Editions, Houghton & Mifflin Publishing, Evian Mineral Water (TBWA)

SELECTED AWARDS
_ Society of Illustrators New York
_ The Hamilton King Award
_ Bologna Book Fair Graphic Prize 1981/1989

SELECTED EXHIBITIONS
_ Retrospective, Musée des Arts Décoratifs, Le Louvre, Paris, 1975
_ Retrospective, Palazzo delle Esposizione, Rome, 1992
_ Retrospective, Library of Congress, Washington DC, 1994
_ Retrospective, Musée Olympique, Lausanne, 1997-1998
_ Prophets and Pretenders, Musée Jenisch, Vevey, 1992

Jean-Philippe Delhomme

1959 born in Paris, France | lives and works in Paris, France
www.jphdelhomme.com

"Paintings in a semi-abstract form, yet accurately figurative, with subjects ranging from fashion and portraits, to a satirical take on culture."

„Ich male in halbabstrakter Form, doch präzise figürlich, und meine Themen reichen von Mode über Porträts bis hin zu einem satirischen Blick auf die Kultur.“

« Des peintures aux formes semi-abstraites et pourtant intensément figuratives, avec de sujets allant de la mode au portrait, un point de vue satirique sur la culture. »

↑   *Clouds, by Ronan & Erwan Bouroullec for Kvadrat*, 2009, Grazia Casa
→   *Alexander McQueen*, Fashion Week 2008, Libération newspaper
→→   *Gallery booth – Miami Art Basel 2008*, 2009, personal work

TOOLS
Gouache on paper, coloured pencils

CLIENTS
Le Bon Marché Rive Gauche, Colette, Interview magazine, GQ, Architectural Digest, Case da Abitare, Stern, Travel & Leisure, Condé Nast Traveller, The New Yorker, Casa Brutus, Barneys, Saab

SELECTED EXHIBITIONS
_Partners & Spade, New York
_Colette, Paris
_James Danziger, New York
_Rocket Gallery, Tokyo
_Institut Français, Berlin

← *Dash Snow*, 2009, personal work
↓ *The Style Guy*, 2009, GQ magazine, USA

↖ *Gallery Booth - Miami Art Basel 2008*, 2009, personal work
← *Design Miami 2008*, 2009, Architectural Digest, France
↘ *Viktor & Rolf*, 2008, Case da Abitare

Isabelle Dervaux

1961 born in Valenciennes, France | lives and works in New York (NY), USA
www.isabelledervaux.com

> *"I like to make people smile, reflect on things, or think. Coming up with ideas and metaphors is the most enjoyable part of my work."*

> *„Ich bringe Menschen gerne zum Lächeln und dazu, sich über die Dinge Gedanken zu machen. Wenn ich mir Ideen und Metaphern einfallen lasse, ist das der Teil meiner Arbeit, der mir am meisten Spaß macht."*

> *« J'aime faire sourire les gens, les faire réfléchir, les faire penser. Suggérer des idées et des métaphores est l'aspect le plus plaisant de mon travail. »*

↑ *The Introvert*, 2005, self-promotion
→ *Give Something Back*, jumbo postcard mailing, 2005
    Art Director: Jorge Salcedo, Communication Group
→→ *Night on the Town*, 2008, ISO, Source Media Inc. Art Director: Jacqueline Rider

TOOLS
Black and white paintbrush, ink, paper, scanner, Adobe Photoshop, Adobe Illustrator

CLIENTS
The New York Times, The Washington Post, John Brown Media, Hachette, Tena, Kraft, ECC

SELECTED EXHIBITIONS
_ CWC Gallery, Tokyo
_ Society of Illustrators

AGENT
Philippe Arnaud
www.philippearnaud.com

CWC
Tokyo, Japan
www.cwctokyo.com

David Despau

1972 born in Madrid, Spain | lives and works in Madrid, Spain
www.despau.com

↑ *3 colours_Black*, 2008, personal work
→ *3 colours_Yellow*, 2008, personal work

"I am fascinated by faces, drawing them realistically or simplifying them almost to abstraction. Composition and rhythm are fundamental to an illustration."

„Mich faszinieren Gesichter ganz besonders: Ich zeichne sie realistisch oder vereinfache sie zu beinahe abstrakten Darstellungen. Komposition und Rhythmus sind die Grundlage einer Illustration."

« J'adore les visages, les dessiner avec réalisme ou les simplifier jusqu'à l'abstraction ou presque. Pour une illustration, la composition et le rythme sont fondamentaux. »

TOOLS
Pen, ballpoint pen, ink, Adobe Photoshop, Adobe Illustrator, Adobe After Effects

CLIENTS
Saatchi & Saatchi, Publicis, Renault, Lamilk magazine, Telefónica, Conde Nast, Beam Global, Jaleo DSGN

Cvendra

Nick Dewar

1973 born in Dundee, UK | lives and works in Laguna Beach (CA), USA
www.nickdewar.com

↑ *Not a Bang but a Squeak*, 2005, Bloomberg
Art Director: Frank Tagariello
→ *Summer Sale*, 2006, Harry Rosen
Art Director: Bob Goulart
→→ *Reducing Your Carbon Footprint*, 2007, Readers Digest UK
Art Directors: Hugh Kyle and Martin Colyer

"Inspired by the way poor quality print-outs of pictures make my own work pale when placed alongside them, I find they also spur me onwards by reminding me how beautiful and rewarding art can be."

„Inspiriert von der Art, wie qualitativ schlechte Ausdrucke von Bildern meine eigenen Arbeiten blass wirken lassen, wenn sie daneben stehen, treibt es mich auch an, denn es erinnert mich daran, wie schön und lohnend Kunst sein kann.“

« Inspiré par la façon dont mon propre travail pâlit de la comparaison avec des tirages d'image de mauvaise qualité, je trouve qu'ils m'incitent aussi à poursuivre en me rappelant à quel point l'art peut être beau et gratifiant. »

TOOLS
Sable paintbrush, illustration board, Flashe acrylic, Cel-Vinyl acrylic paints, Wacom tablet, wood, fabric, rusty electrical objects

CLIENTS
Elle Decor, Forbes, Harpers Bazaar, GQ, The New York Times, Newsweek, Playboy, Time magazine, The Wall Street Journal, The Guardian, The Times (London), The Observer, Bloomsbury, Random House

SELECTED AWARDS
_ Society of Publication Designers 2000/2004
_ British Association of Illustrators 2004
_ Society of Newspaper Design 1997
_ HOW magazine 1996

SELECTED EXHIBITIONS
_ Manifest Hope, Democratic National Convention, 2008/2009
_ Nomonotono, Madrid, 2008
_ Images (traveling exhibition), UK, 1998–2000/2004–2006
_ Young Guns II/III, Art Directors Club, New York, 1998/2001

AGENT
Kate Larkworthy Artist Representation
New York, USA
www.larkworthy.com

Eastwing
London, UK
www.eastwing.co.uk

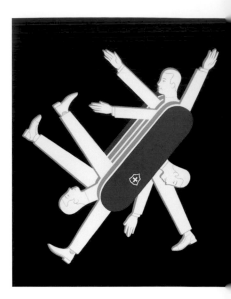

↑   *Conspicuous Consumption*, 2001, Bloomberg. Art Director: Beatrice MacDonald
↗   *PDA*, 2003, EDesign magazine
→   *Dancing Girl*, 2007, personal work

Rainman, 2003, Japanese Airlines magazine
Lolly, 2008, S magazine
Trashwoman, 2005, personal work

Nicholas Di Genova

1981 born in Belleville, Ontario, Canada | lives and works in Toronto, Ontario, Canada
www.mediumphobic.com

*"I document the flora
and fauna that may or
may not exist in this world."*

„Ich dokumentiere Flora und Fauna,
wie sie in der Welt vielleicht real
existieren oder auch nicht."

« Je répertorie la flore et la faune,
celle qui existe et celle qui n'existe
pas en ce monde. »

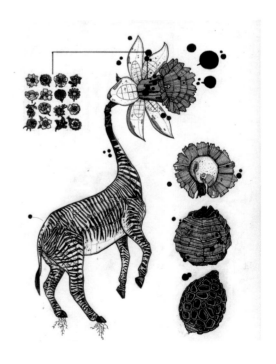

↑ *Siamese Chicken-Hounds*, 2006, personal work
→ *Mammal/Botany Hybrid #1*, 2008, personal work
→→ *Bi-Necked Amphibious Climber*, 2006, personal work

TOOLS
Pen, ink, animation paint

CLIENTS
Whitney Museum of American Art, Coleccao Madeira Corporate Services, Portugal, Fidelity Investments

SELECTED EXHIBITIONS
_ Die Young, Intoxicated Demons Gallery, Berlin, 2008
_ Birds are Terrifying Creatures, LE Gallery, Toronto, 2007
_ Due West of the Happy-Lake Hills, LE Gallery, Toronto, 2005
_ Death From Below: The Upper Layers of the Hades Geofront, Fredericks & Freiser, New York, 2006
_ At the Water's Edge, LE Gallery, Toronto, 2004

AGENT
Fredericks & Freiser Gallery New York, USA
fredericksfreisergallery.com

Galerie Dukan and Hourdequin Marseilles, France
www.dukanhourdequin.com

LE Gallery
Toronto, Canada
www.le-gallery.ca

Mark Dickson

1976 born in Nottingham, UK | lives and works in Nottingham, UK
www.i-am-mark.com

↑   *Stephen Fry*, 2009, personal work
→   *Bat for Lashes*, 2009, personal work
→→ *Lily*, 2009, personal work

"Lately I have been returning to the hand-drawn, using printing ink, watercolour, spray-paint, acrylic… anything I can get my hands on really, to satisfy the desire to connect physically with my materials and with the process."

„Kürzlich bin ich wieder zum Zeichnen mit der Hand zurückgekehrt und setze Tusche, Wasserfarben, Sprüh- oder Acrylfarben ein … alles, was ich real in die Hand nehmen kann, um meinen Wunsch nach einer physischen Verbindung mit dem Material und dem Prozess zu befriedigen."

« Dernièrement, je suis revenu au dessin à la main, et j'utilise l'encre d'imprimerie, l'aquarelle, la peinture en aérosol, la peinture acrylique… n'importe quoi que je puisse vraiment tenir en main, pour satisfaire mon désir d'être en contact physique avec les matériaux et la création. »

TOOLS
Watercolour, ink, fountain pen, spray paint, Adobe Photoshop, Adobe Illustrator, hand drawings, imagery, textures, scanner

CLIENTS
Virgin, Sainsbury's, Nokia, Tesco, Firetrap, Emap, Observer Review, Digital Creative Arts

SELECTED AWARDS
_ Brighton Festival Fringe Visual Art Prize 2005

SELECTED EXHIBITIONS
_ Printworks, solo exhibition, New Stein Hotel, Brighton, 2005

AGENT
Folio
London, UK
www.folioart.co.uk

Glauco Diogenes

1979 born in São Paulo, Brazil | lives and works in São Paulo, Brazil, New York (NY), USA, and Barcelona, Spain
www.glaucodiogenes.com.br

↑ *Wall Street*, 2006, Editora Globo, Época Negócios magazine
→ *Cow Parade RIO 2007*, website and exhibition, 2007, Cow Parade Holdings Corporation / Tok&Stok

"I have a specific way of drawing using vector software. I am not limited to a particular style or type of expression. And I'm always looking for new ways to play."

„Meine Arbeitsweise beim Zeichnen ist speziell, weil ich Vektorsoftware einsetze. Ich bin nicht auf einen bestimmten Stil oder eine spezielle Art des Ausdrucks festgelegt. Außerdem suche ich immer nach neuen Wegen, um zu spielen."

« J'ai une façon particulière d'utiliser le logiciel de dessin vectoriel. Je ne me limite pas à un style ou un type d'expression particulier. Et je suis toujours en quête de nouvelles manières de jouer. »

TOOLS
Vectorial illustration, Adobe Photoshop, pencil, paper, digital camera, Wacom tablet

CLIENTS
Superinteressante, Vogue, Accessorize London, Absolut, Greenpeace, Globo, Marcelo Rosenbaum, Computer Arts Brazil, Zupi, Banco Santander, Chrysler, Gazeta Mercantil, Maximidia, Abril

SELECTED AWARDS
_ Society of Illustrators Illustration Annual 2006/2008
_ Lürzer's Archive 200 Best Illustrators Worldwide 07–08
_ Communication Arts Illustration Annual 2005
_ Prêmio Abril de Jornalismo 2004 (finalist)

SELECTED EXHIBITIONS
_ Absolut Brasil, São Paulo, 2007
_ Cow Parade, Rio de Janeiro, 2007
_ Toy Art Chrysler, São Paulo/ Rio de Janeiro, 2008
_ Greenpeace Ocean, Brazil, 2008

_ Ilustrando em Revista (Editora Abril), São Paulo/ Rio de Janeiro/Brasília/ Minas Gerais, 2005

Chairs from Glauco Diogenes

↑   *WGSN Lounge – São Paulo Fashion Week*, wallpaper, 2008, WGSN, Rosenbaum Design

Véronique Dorey

1963 born in Le Mans, France | lives and works in Paris, France

↑ *Rendez-vous*, "A Time For Love" paintings, 2008, personal work
↗ *Highway to Hell*, "A Time For Love" paintings, 2005, personal work
→ *Illicit Dreams*, "A Time For Love" paintings, 2006, personal work

*"Somewhere between Chris Ware, the lowbrow California scene,
and the golden age of publicity illustration."* — *Laurent Zorzin, Arts Factory*

„Irgendwo zwischen Chris Ware, der kalifornischen Lowbrow-Szene und dem goldenen Zeitalter der Reklameillustration."

« Niché quelque part entre Chris Ware, la scène low brow californienne et l'âge d'or de l'illustration publicitaire. »

TOOLS	CLIENTS	SELECTED EXHIBITIONS	AGENT
Acrylic on paper	Arts Factory, Humanoïdes Associés, Hachette, Albin Michel	_Sweet Heart, Arts Factory, Galerie Nomade, Paris, 2005 _Arts Factory Summer Show, Espace Beaurepaire, Paris, 2007 _Cité du Livre, Aix en Provence, France, 2008 _Welcome to my Dollhouse, Espace Beaurepaire, Paris, 2009	La Superette Paris, France www.lasuperette.com

HIGHWAY TO HELL

FOR BETTER OR FOR WORSE

a time for Love

ILLICIT DREAMS

a time for Love

LOW FIDELITY

Valero Doval

1978 born in Valencia, Spain | lives and works in London, UK
www.valerodoval.com

"My work is a mix of illustration and collage filled with colour, wit, and style. It's a combination of vintage imagery, nature, and delicate handwork."

„Meine Arbeit ist eine Mischung aus Illustration und Collagen, voller Farben, Esprit und Stil. Es ist eine Kombination aus altmodischen Bildern, der Natur und feiner Handarbeit."

« Mon travail est un mélange d'illustration et de collage, truffé de couleur, d'astuce et de style. C'est une combinaison d'imagerie ancienne, de nature et de délicat travail à la main. »

↑ *Good looking at work*, 2008, Diego magazine, Sweden
→ *Drawers series #2*, 2008, personal work
→→ *Woodland*, T-shirt illustration, 2008, Timberland

TOOLS
Collage, pen, pencil, paper, computer

CLIENTS
The New York Times, Kenzo, Timberland, Wallpaper, Orange, Panasonic, MacUser, Enroute magazine, Teachers magazine, Building magazine

SELECTED AWARDS
_Creative Futures 2005, Creative Review magazine
_3x3 magazine

SELECTED EXHIBITIONS
_Royal College of Art, London, 2007
_Dray Walk Gallery, London, 2008
_Mr Pink Gallery, Valencia, Spain, 2008
_PUB, Stockholm, 2008
_American Book Center, Amsterdam, 2008

AGENT
NU Agency
Stockholm, Sweden
www.nuagency.se

Christina Drejenstam

1977 born in Gothenburg, Sweden | lives and works in Stockholm, Sweden
www.drejenstam.se

"My illustrations are modern yet classical – they are both simplified and rich in detail at the same time."

„*Meine Illustrationen sind modern und doch klassisch. Sie vereinfachen und sind gleichzeitig auch detailreich.*"

« *Mes illustrations sont modernes et pourtant classiques – elles sont à la fois simples et riches de détails.* »

↑   *Untitled*, 2008, personal work
←   *Untitled*, T-shirt illustration, 2007, WESC
→   *Untitled*, advertising, 2007, Lindex

TOOLS
Pen, pencil, watercolour,
spray paint, Adobe Photoshop

CLIENTS
Nike, Renault, WESC,
Oceans Terminal, Audemars
Piguet, Nokia

SELECTED AWARDS
_Society for News Design
Annual Creative Competition

AGENT
Peppercookies
London, UK
www.peppercookies.com

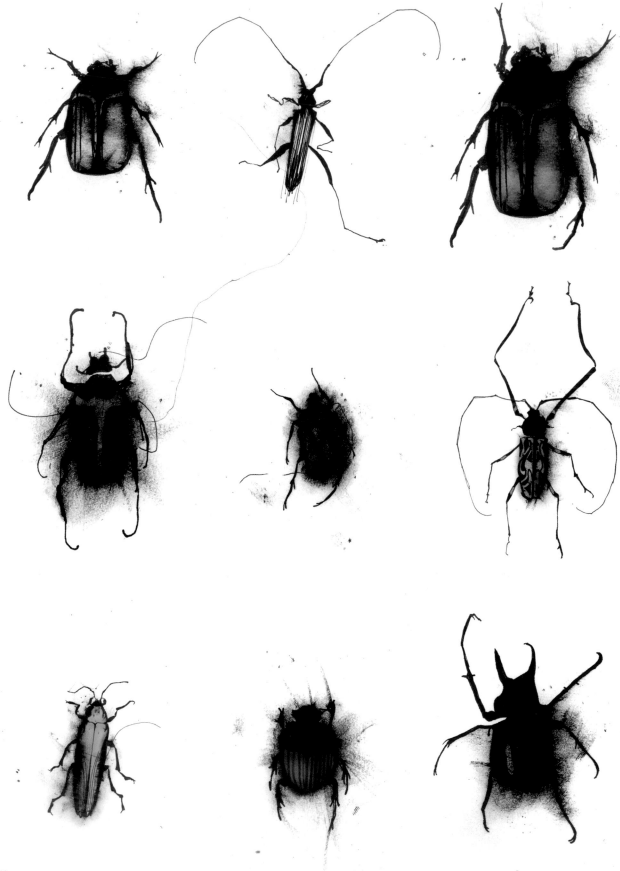

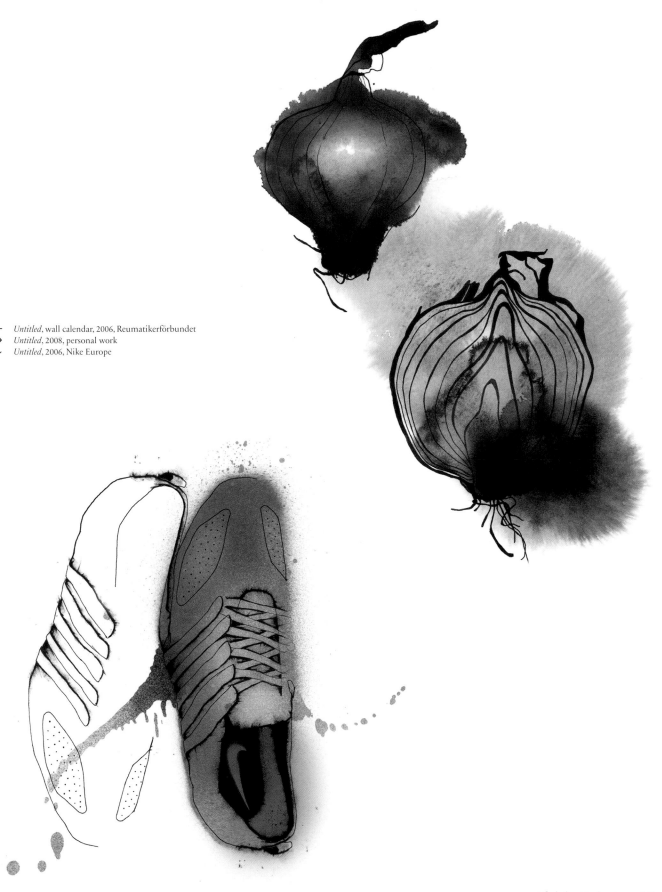

Robin Eley

1978 born in London, UK | lives and works in Tranmere, Australia
www.levycreative.com

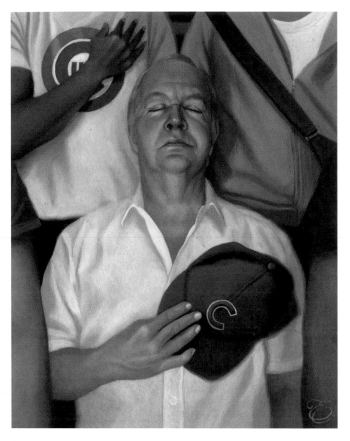

"I combine traditional techniques with contemporary points of view. My work is relatable in its realism, but challenging in its concepts and complexity."

„Ich kombiniere traditionelle Techniken mit aktuellen Sichtweisen. Meine Arbeiten können durch ihren Realismus gut zugeordnet werden, sind aber hinsichtlich der Konzepte und der Komplexität auch eine Herausforderung."

« J'allie les techniques traditionnelles et les points de vue contemporains. Mon travail est racontable par son réalisme, mais provocateur par ses concepts et sa complexité. »

↑   *Death and Baseball*, 2009, North Shore magazine
→   *Obama vs. Clinton*, 2008, Portfolio magazine
→→ *Wolfmother*, 2007, self-promotional

TOOLS
Acrylic on masonite or illustration board, golden or Liquitex acrylics with Liquitex Matte Medium, Filbert, hog-hair bristle brushes, small synthetics for detail

CLIENTS
Time magazine, Disney, Village Voice, The Wall Street Journal, Revolver, Vibe, Men's Fitness, Clemenger BBDO, The Week, The Deal, Guitar World, XXL magazine, Miami New Times

SELECTED AWARDS
_ Society of Illustrators 49/51
_ Communication Arts 48
_ Rip it Up magazine Emerging Artist Award 2008
_ Society of Illustrators 49 Advertising 2007

SELECTED EXHIBITIONS
_ Solo Exhibition, Out of Context, South Australian Living Artists Festival, 2008
_ Society of Illustrators 51, Book and Editorial Exhibition, 2009

AGENT
Levy Creative Management
New York, USA
www.levycreative.com

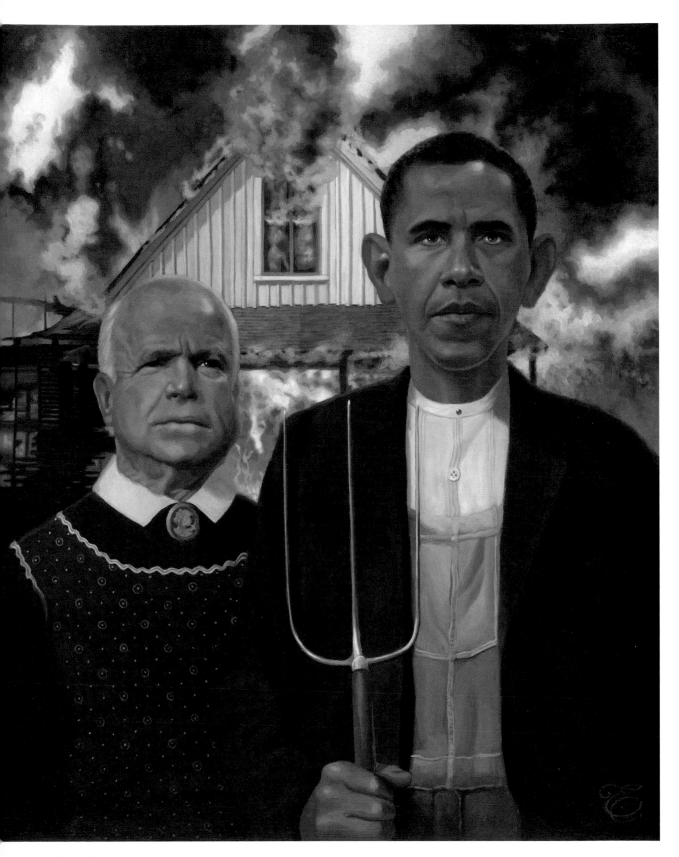

Presidential Gothic, 2008, The Week magazine
Displacement, 2008, Memphis magazine

Enkeling

1973 born in De Veenhoop, Netherlands | lives and works in Amsterdam, Netherlands
www.enkeling.nl

↑   *Autechre*, 2008, personal work
→   *Branded*, 2008, personal work

"Although my work might seem hard to define to some, a curiosity about what's over the horizon could just be the very thing that defines it."

„Obwohl meine Arbeit für manche schwer definierbar erscheint, könnte man sie doch genau dadurch beschreiben, dass sie von der Neugier auf etwas hinter dem Horizont angetrieben wird."

« Bien qu'il puisse sembler difficile à certains de le définir, mon travail pourrait bien s'expliquer par une curiosité pour ce tout qu'il y a au-delà de l'horizon. »

TOOLS
Pen, pencil, marker, brush, paint, ink, Ecoline, drawing tablet, digital camera, paper, scanner, Adobe Photoshop, Adobe Illustrator

CLIENTS
Blaadje, Bright, COC, Custo Barcelona, Defiant.tv, Dust, Geldgids, Hoofdproductschap Akkerbouw, Interpolis, Vara's Kassa, Kop of Munt, La Vie en Rose, Maandag, OOM, het Parool, Shell, YouTube, Zin

↑ *Artificials, Man-mades*, 2008, personal work
↗ *San Francisco*, 2007, La Vie en Rose magazine
→ *Cat/Woman*, 2008, personal work
← *Ben Kremer*, 2007, personal work

Randall Enos

1936 born in New Bedford (MA), USA | lives and works in Easton (CT), USA
www.randallenos.com

"*The expressionistic quality
of the cartoon medium,
with its exaggerations of color
and form, has served me perfectly
in making my statements
about man and his world.*"

„*Die expressionistische Qualität des Mediums Cartoons
mit seinen übertriebenen Formen und Farben eignet
sich für mich ganz hervorragend, wenn ich meine
Aussagen über die Menschen und ihre Welt treffe.*"

« *La qualité expressionniste du dessin animé,
avec ses outrances de couleur et de forme,
a parfaitement servi mon propos : exposer mes
vues sur l'homme et son monde.* »

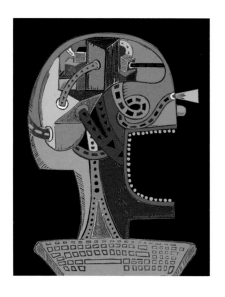

↑   *King Pest* , illustration of an Edgar Allan Poe story, 1987, personal work
→   *Trusted Computing*, magazine cover, 2006, Networker magazine
→→ *Rewriting the Script*, magazine cover, 2008, Rethinking Schools
     Art Director: Patrick JB Flynn

TOOLS
Linocut, coloured papers,
digital colour

CLIENTS
The New York Times, The Wall
Street Journal, Reader's Digest,
Mother Jones, TIME, U.S.
News, Forbes, Fortune

SELECTED AWARDS
_Cannes Festival 1964
_Association of Small
magazines
_Society of Illustrators New
York 2007

SELECTED EXHIBITIONS
_Artists Against the War
(Vietnam), Society of
Illustrators
_Artists Against the Iraq War,
Society of Illustrators
_200 Years of American
Illustration

_Illustrating the Sea
(Curator + Exhibitor), Mystic
Seaport Mystic, Connecticut
_Politics '08, Society of
Illustrators

AGENT
Folio
London, UK
www.folioart.co.uk

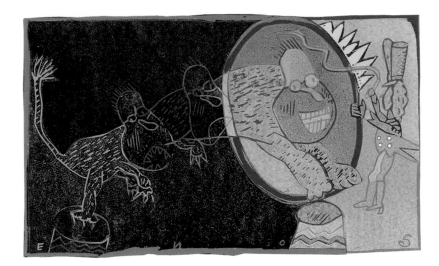

← *Frida Kahlo*, personal work
→ *Good Boss, Bad Boss*, 2007,
   Smith College Alumni magazine
↘ *Can of Beans*, inspired by the lyric
   of a Tom Waits song, 2006,
   self-promotion

Erotic Dragon

1970 born in Tokyo, Japan | lives and works in Tokyo, Japan
www.eroticdragon.com

*"Everything the eye can see is
a source of creation for me.
The world is brimming with shapes
and colour, it never bores me."*

*„Alles, was das Auge sehen kann, wird für mich
zur Inspirationsquelle. Die Welt strotzt vor Farben
und Formen und wird mir nie langweilig."*

*« Tout ce que l'œil peut voir est pour moi une
source de créativité. Le monde déborde de formes
et de couleurs, il ne m'ennuie jamais. »*

↑   *Jesus and Buddha*, book cover, 2007, Kodansha
→   *Calices de fleurs*, 2007, personal work
→→ *Amber*, 2008, personal work

TOOLS
Sketches, pencil, paper, Adobe
Illustrator, Adobe Photoshop

CLIENTS
Kodansha Publishing, Shinsei
Publishing, Japan Interior
Industry Association, Zero
First Design, Area Design,
London Transport,
Die Gestalten Verlag

SELECTED EXHIBITIONS
_Hotel Wonder, La Perla,
Milan, 2006
_Spread the Lead, Gallery
Hanahou, New York, 2008

AGENT
CWC International
New York, USA
www.cwc-i.com

CWC
Tokyo, Japan
www.cwctokyo.com

Pier Fichefeux

1976 born in Paris, France | lives and works in Paris, France, and New York (NY), USA
www.pier-f.biz

"My work is a mix of Asian influences, the contemplation of nature, and storytelling. It's all about textures, pattern, and a confusion of layers."

„Meine Arbeit ist eine Mischung aus asiatischen Einflüssen, Naturbetrachtung und dem Erzählen von Geschichten. Dabei geht es stets um Texturen, Muster und die Verschmelzung von Schichten."

« Mon travail est un mélange d'influences asiatiques, de contemplation de la nature et de contes. Tout tourne autour des textures, des motifs et d'une confusion de couches. »

↑   *Untitled*, 2006, Publicis Drugstore, Paris
→   *Untitled*, 2006, Publicis Drugstore, Paris
→→ *Untitled*, 2006, Publicis Drugstore, Paris

TOOLS
Adobe Photoshop,
Wacom tablet

CLIENTS
Wallpaper, Uomini Gufi

SELECTED EXHIBITIONS
_ Fabrica Les Yeux Ouverts,
Pompidou Center, Paris
_ Exposif Wallpapers, Maxalot
Gallery
_ A Cat A Forest A Condom
Painting, Bodhi Gallery,
London

_ Ritratti Neri Fabrica Feature,
Lisbon
_ You and I And Dominoes
Painting, Sette Chiese,
Bologna, Italy

AGENT
Talkie Walkie
Paris, France
www.talkiewalkie.tw

Finger Industries

2002 founded in Sheffield, UK
www.fingerindustries.co.uk

↑   *Plaything*, 2008, self-promotion
→   *Sushi Bar*, in-store brochure, 2008, Lloyds TSB Commercial Banking

"We are a group of artists with a single goal, loads of imagination and 3-D skills,
too much coffee, and a track record of making clients very happy indeed."

„Wir haben als Künstlergruppe ein gemeinsames Ziel und eine unbändige Vorstellungskraft, viel Ahnung von 3-D,
trinken zuviel Kaffee, und unsere Kunden sind mit unserer Arbeit wirklich glücklich und zufrieden."

« Nous sommes un groupe d'artistes partageant un seul et même but, de l'imagination et du savoir-faire à revendre
en matière de 3-D, beaucoup trop de café et un répertoire bourré de clients hyper contents. »

TOOLS
Pencils, Adobe Photoshop,
Discreet 3ds Max

CLIENTS
Lloyds TSB, TMW, Hamleys of
London, Brahm, Random
House, Tesco, Hodder
Headline, Guardian Weekend,
Bank of Scotland, Scottish
Media Group, Pulse Films,
WAA, Sunday Times

Vince Fraser

1972 born in London, UK | lives and works in London, UK
www.vincefraser.com

↑   *Work and Play*, 2009, Sleek magazine
→   *Sin City*, website, posters, flyers, and all promotional material, 2009, Urban Fashion Week

"Implementing a wide variety of elements from photographs to typography and vector illustration, my compositions conceal a broad palette."

„In meinen Kompositionen baue ich vielfältige Elemente aus Fotografie über Typografie bis hin zur Vektorillustration in meine Palette ein."

« J'emploie un large éventail d'éléments, de la photo à la typographie en passant par l'illustration vectorielle, et mes compositions couvrent donc une très large palette. »

TOOLS
Adobe Photoshop, Adobe Illustrator, 3D Studio Max, digital camera, scanner, Wacom tablet

CLIENTS
British Airways, Tiger Beer, BBC, PC World, T-Mobile, Getty Images, Co-Operative Bank, Hugo Boss, Dow Jones Hong Kong, Acer Computers

SELECTED AWARDS
_Royal Society of Arts

Owen Freeman

1978 born in Houston (TX), USA | lives and works in Los Angeles (CA), USA
www.owenfreeman.com

"My process is about creating a sense of drama in visual storytelling."

„In meinem Prozess geht es mir darum, ein Gefühl für Dramatik im visuellen Geschichtenerzählen zu schaffen.“

« Donner un sens dramatique à la narration visuelle, voilà ce que je cherche. »

↑   *Birds*, 2008, personal work
→   *Get Up*, 2008, personal work
→→ *Aqualad*, 2007, personal work

TOOLS
Ink, watercolour,
Adobe Photoshop

CLIENTS
Scholastic, Runner's World,
Aeroflot Airlines

Sean Freeman

1986 born in Gibraltar, UK | lives and works in London, UK

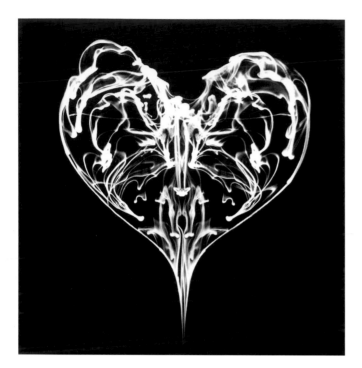

← *Ink Heart*, T-shirt, 2008, Iron Fist
→ *What it Feels Like*, 2008, Esquire magazine
↓ *Ink Lady*, 2008, personal work

"I produce a sort of semi-photographic type of treatments and illustrations, constantly looking for new and interesting ways of treating and creating images."

„Wenn ich produziere, arbeite ich gewissermaßen semi-fotografisch mit Illustrationen, wobei ich immer nach neuen und interessanten Möglichkeiten suche, Bilder zu bearbeiten und zu erschaffen."

« J'invente toutes sortes de procédés et d'illustrations semi photographiques, en cherchant constamment des manières nouvelles et intéressantes de traiter et créer des images. »

TOOLS
Digital camera, scanner, Adobe Photoshop

CLIENTS
The New York Times magazine, The Guardian, Esquire magazine, VH1, Harper Collins, BON magazine, Iron Fist

AGENT
Colagene
Montreal, Canada
Paris, France
www.colagene.com

← *Sophie*, 2009, BON magazine
Photography by Rafael Stahelin
→ *Lorem Ipsum*, 2008, personal work
↓ *A Little Flutter*, 2008, BD Network

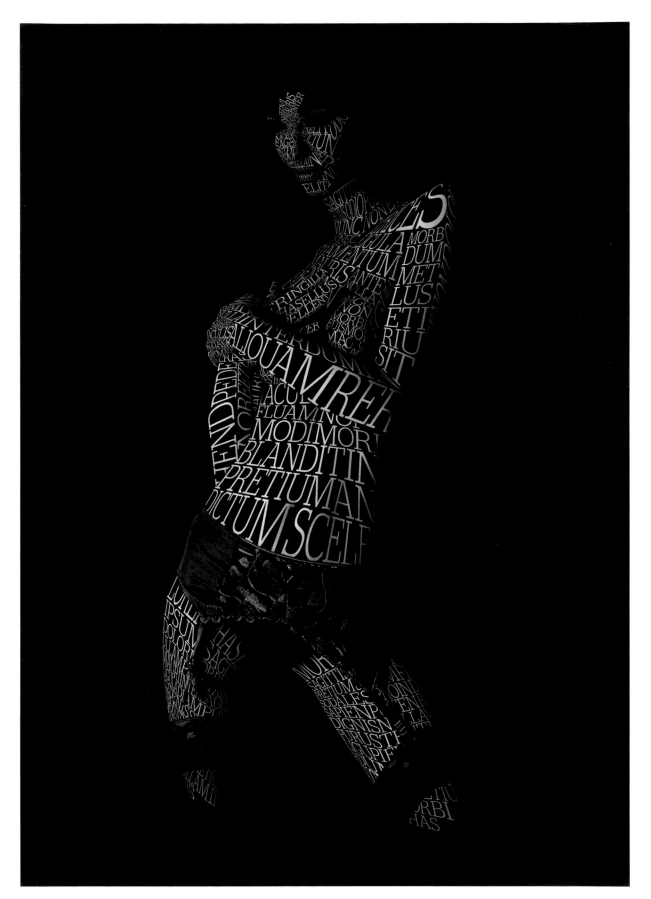

Miriam Frei

1978 born in Schaffhausen, Switzerland | lives and works in Zurich, Switzerland, and Rotterdam, Netherlands
www.miriamfrei.ch

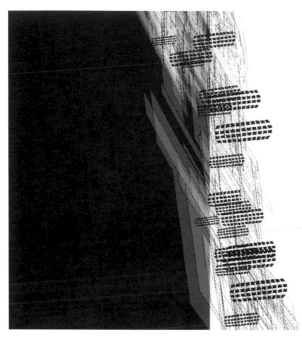

↑ *Seasons*, 2008, personal work
→ *21 houses*, 2008, personal work
→→ *Journey Through the Past*, book project, 2008

"Illustrations are like glass between thoughts and words."

*„Illustrationen sind Glas
zwischen Gedanken und Worten.“*

*« Les illustrations sont un peu comme
une vitre entre la pensée et les mots. »*

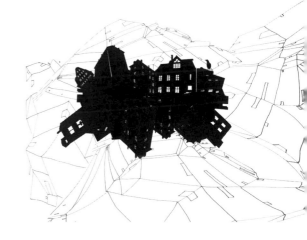

TOOLS
Black pencil, paper,
scanner, Adobe Photoshop,
Adobe Illustrator

CLIENTS
City of Zurich

SELECTED AWARDS
_ Illustrative Award
_ Kaspar Diener Award

SELECTED EXHIBITIONS
_ Illustrative Zurich, 2008
_ Kaspar Diener Award
Exhibition, 2008

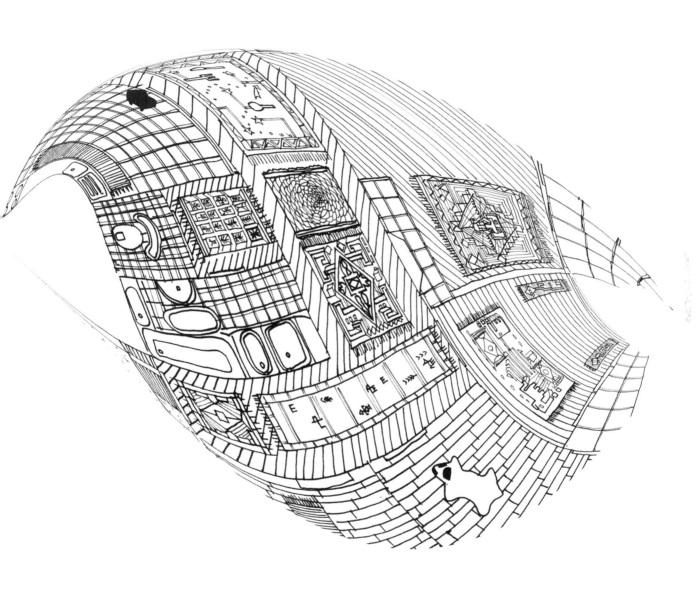

Hope Gangloff

1974 born in Amityville (NY), USA | lives and works in New York (NY), USA
www.hopegangloff.com

← *Hipsters for Blackbook*, 2005, Blackbook
→ *Staten Island Makes Its Case*, 2006, personal work
↓ *A light*, 2006, personal work

"Drawing is the way I relate to my peers, family, and the world around me – be it to disarm, provoke, tease, flatter, or explain things."

„Zeichnen ist die Art, mich mit Gleichgesinnten, meiner Familie und der Welt um mich herum in Beziehung zu setzen – sei es, um zu entwaffnen, zu provozieren, zu reizen, zu schmeicheln oder Dinge zu erklären."

« Le dessin est ma façon à moi de me rapporter à mes semblables, à ma famille, au monde qui m'entoure – que ce soit pour désarçonner, provoquer, agacer, flatter ou raconter des choses. »

TOOLS
Pen and ink on paper

CLIENTS
New Yorker, New York Times, Vice New York magazine, Tank, I-D, Guardian UK, Grolsch Beer, Dazed & Confused, Cosmo France, GQ France, Soho House magazine, Vanity Fair, Pentagram

SELECTED EXHIBITIONS
_Susan Inglett Gallery, New York, 2008
_Susan Inglett Gallery, New York, 2007
_Richard Heller Gallery, Los Angeles, 2008
_Endemica Gallery, Rome, 2008

AGENT
Art Department
New York, USA
www.art-dept.com

← *Masnyjs*, 2008, personal work

Theo Gennitsakis

1982 born in Thessaloniki, Greece | lives and works in Paris, France, Athens, Greece, and London, UK
www.theogennitsakis.com

*"A little kitsch, some colours,
some details… many objects,
and a few messages in the artworks."*

„Ein bisschen Kitsch, ein paar Farben, einige Details …
viele Objekte und in den Kunstwerken ein paar Botschaften."

« Un rien de kitsch, quelques couleurs, quelques détails…
beaucoup d'objets, et des messages par-ci par-là sur les dessins. »

↑   *Untitled*, 2009, personal work
→   *Untitled*, 2009, personal work
→→ *Untitled*, 2009, personal work

TOOLS
Pen, paper, Adobe Photoshop,
Adobe Illustrator, photography,
Wacom tablet

CLIENTS
Nike, Kai, Clark magazine

SELECTED AWARDS
_ The FWA
_ New York Festival
_ Cannes Lions 2007

SELECTED EXHIBITIONS
_ Citadium, Paris
_ Game Paused, London
_ Galerie Nouvelle, Paris
_ La Secu, Lille

AGENT
Smart Magna
Athens, Greece
www.smartmagna.com

Michael Gillette

1970 born in Swansea, UK | lives and works in San Francisco (CA), USA

"I like to start with an idea, and voice it in a manner that expresses it most forcefully, rather than working in a catch-all style or medium."

„Ich beginne gerne mit einer Idee und artikuliere sie auf eine Weise, die sie möglichst kraftvoll ausdrückt, anstatt in einem allumfassenden Stil oder Medium zu arbeiten."

« J'aime partir d'une idée, et la formuler d'une manière capable de l'exprimer avec force, plutôt que d'user d'un style ou d'un procédé fourre-tout. »

↑ *Mantis*, 2008, personal work
→ *Mother Theresa*, 2008, The Guardian
→→ *Embroidery*, Beat #3 "The Gypsy Dream Book", 2006, Heart

TOOLS
Watercolour, pencil, coloured pencil, acrylic, collage, computer

CLIENTS
Penguin, Microsoft, Levi's, Nokia, Esquire, Greenpeace, Apple, Capitol Records, MTV, Sony, ESPN, Old Navy, Warner Bros, Orange, Natwest, GQ, New York Times, Wallpaper, WPP, Chronicle Books

SELECTED EXHIBITIONS
_ Solo exhibition, Levi's flagship store, San Francisco, 2005
_ Little Angels solo exhibition, Parlor Projects Gallery, San Francisco, 2002
_ Solo exhibition, The Groucho Club, London, 2000
_ Solo exhibition, The Groucho Club, London, 1997

AGENT
Heart
London, UK
www.heartagency.com

Heart USA
New York, USA
www.heartagency.com

↑ *Bond Back Catalogue*, 14 book covers, 2008, Penguin Books / Ian Fleming Estate
→ *Clearification.com*, viral website, 2007, Microsoft

Carlo Giovani

1977 born in Santa Maria, Rio Grande do Sul, Brazil | lives and works in São Paulo, Brazil
www.carlogiovani.com

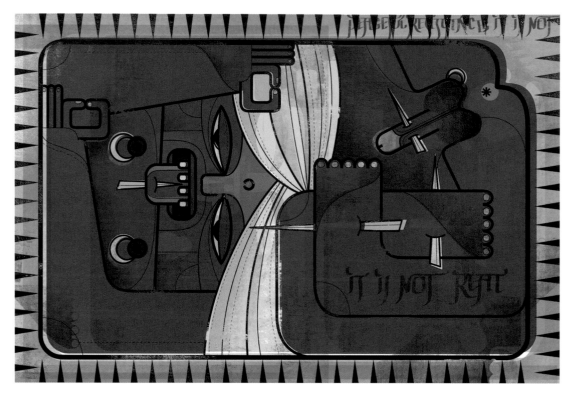

↑ *It Is Not Real*, 2007, S/N magazine
↗ *Rice Flakes – Feed Your Monsters*, poster, 2007, Simples magazine
→ *Chinese Tea Box*, 2006, self-promotion

*"I like to work with different media and techniques, mixing
them to create new ways of representing ideas and concepts."*

*„Ich arbeite gerne mit verschiedenen Medien und Techniken und mische sie untereinander,
um neue Möglichkeiten zu schaffen, wie man Ideen und Konzepte verdeutlichen kann."*

*« J'aime travailler avec différents médias et techniques, les mêler pour créer
de nouvelles façons de représenter idées et concepts. »*

TOOLS
Pen, paper, Wacom tablet,
Adobe Photoshop,
Adobe Illustrator,

CLIENTS
Nike, Pepsi, Coca-Cola, Ford,
Elma Chips, Lacta, LG, TIM,
Kibon, MTV Brazil, Havaianas,
McDonald's

SELECTED AWARDS
_ Malofiej Infographics Award
2006
_ Prêmio Esso de Jornalismo
2008
_ Max Feffer Award 2008
_ Prêmio Abril de Jornalismo
_ PROMAX&BDA Latin
America

SELECTED EXHIBITIONS
_ 1/2 Dúzia de Idéias Expostas,
solo exhibition, Pastik Gallery,
São Paulo, 2008
_ 8th Biennial of Graphic
Design, ADG, São Paulo, 2006
_ Ilustrando em Revista, Brazil,
2005-2008

Stéphane Goddard

1968 born in Chambéry, France | lives and works in Paris, France
www.stephanegoddard.com

"I try to paint sensual, elegant, and modern pictures which are full of impact. I want them to produce 'direct emotions'. Emotion is a universal language."

„Ich versuche, sinnliche, elegante und moderne Bilder zu malen, die möglichst schlagkräftig und effektvoll sind. Ich will, dass sie ‚direkte Emotionen' bewirken. Emotionen sind als Sprache universell."

« J'essaie de peindre des images modernes, élégantes, sensuelles, et pleines de force. Je veux qu'elles produisent des ‹ émotions directes ›. L'émotion est un langage universel. »

← *Tasty Girl*, 2007, wall poster, Attractive concept store
→ *Maki Drum*, exhibition, 2004, Citadium

TOOLS
Gouache, type, photos, scanner, Adobe Photoshop, Adobe Illustrator, Corel Painter

CLIENTS
Nike, Louis Vuitton, Club Med, PPR, Elle, Citadium, Ware magazine, Roxy/Quiksilver, Marie Claire Group, Klay, Télérama

SELECTED AWARDS
_ Rose Advertising Awards 2006
_ French Art Directors Club Awards
_ Angouleme Festival

SELECTED EXHIBITIONS
_ No Standard Exhibition, Citadium & Stade de France
_ Qee Exhibition, Colette/Christie's, France
_ Fukuoka Race Exhibition, Japan
_ Sketches, Musée des Beaux Arts de Lyon, France

AGENT
Agent002
Paris, France
www.agent002.com

Agent Double
Tokyo, Japan
www.agentdouble.com

Good Wives and Warriors

2007 founded in Glasgow, UK | based in Glasgow, UK, and Melbourne, Australia
www.goodwivesandwarriors.co.uk

> *"Collaboration is an important element in our process. We work together on the same drawing or painting, splicing imagery and reacting to each other's ideas. A sort of spontaneous collaboration."*

„Kollaboration ist in unserem Prozess ein wichtiges Element. Wir arbeiten gemeinsam an unseren Zeichnungen oder Gemälden, fügen die Bilder zusammen und reagieren auf Ideen der anderen – eine Art spontane Kollaboration."

« La collaboration est un élément majeur de notre manière de procéder. Nous travaillons ensemble, sur la même peinture ou le même dessin, à mettre bout à bout les images et à réagir aux idées des autres. Une sorte de collaboration spontanée. »

↑ *Mountain Pump*, War Club, Appetite Gallery, Buenos Aires, 2008, personal work
→ *The Sprezzatura Maze*, 2007, Gallery +44 141, Glasgow
→→ *Print #2*, Illustrative exhibition, 2008, personal work
↓↓ *World of Stuff*, 2008, personal work

TOOLS
Fine liners, felt-tip pens, paper, Adobe Photoshop, Adobe Illustrator, blackboard paint, posca pens

CLIENTS
Swatch, MTV, Fake magazine, Amelia's magazine, Jane Wentworth Associates, The Glasgow School of Art, Urban Outfitters, Comme des Garçons, The Glasgow City Marketing Bureau

SELECTED AWARDS
_The Young Illustrators Award (finalist) 2008

SELECTED EXHIBITIONS
_Illustrative International 09, Zurich, 2008
_I Am Not a Fucking Princess, I am the King, The Appetite Gallery, Buenos Aires, Argentina, 2008
_Euro Vision, The Bottle Capp Gallery, San Francisco, 2008
_Incredible Permanent Gains, The Krets Gallery, Malmo, Sweden, 2008
_The Sprezzatura Maze, +44 141 Gallery, Glasgow, 2007

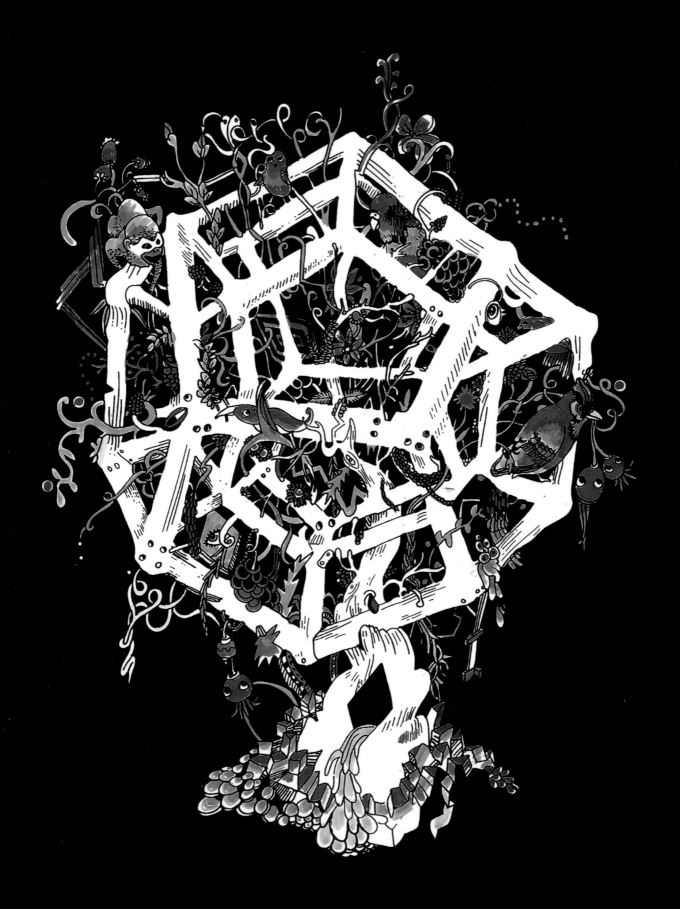

Rodney Alan Greenblat

1960 born in San Francisco (CA), USA | lives and works in New York (NY), USA
www.whimsyload.com

↑   *Self vs. Animal Instinct*, 2003, Whimsyload.com Gallery
→   *Man Buying a Quilt*, 2005, "Elemental" exhibition, Art Print Japan, Graphic's Station Gallery Chain

"My work is a continuing experiment to make beautiful and surprising forms that express something joyous and profound."

„Meine Arbeit ist ein andauerndes Experiment, um schöne und überraschende Formen zu schaffen, die Fröhliches und Hintergründiges ausdrücken."

« Mon travail est une perpétuelle tentative de créer des formes belles et surprenantes capables d'exprimer quelque chose de radieux et de profond. »

TOOLS
Acrylic, watercolour, pastel, wooden multi-material construction, Corel Painter, Adobe Illustrator, Adobe Photoshop, Adobe Flash

CLIENTS
Vanity Fair, The New York Times, Child magazine, Entertainment Weekly, The New Yorker, Nickelodeon, Majesco Entertainment, Toyota, Minolta, Fuji TV, Sony

SELECTED AWARDS
_ Platinum Award
_ Macworld magazine 1992

SELECTED EXHIBITIONS
_ Rodney Alan Greenblat, Gracie Mansion Gallery, New York, 1983
_ Whitney Museum (Biennial Exhibition), New York, 1985
_ Elemental, Art Print Japan Galleries, Tokyo, 2007
_ Reality and Imagination, Two Taste Treats in One, Museum of Art, Penn State University, 1987
_ Land Ho! The Mythic World of Rodney A. Greenblat, Chrysler Museum, Norfolk Virginia, 1992

AGENT
Tak Iwayoshi
Tokyo, Japan
www.interlink-planning.com

Rodney Alan Greenblat

Sophie Griotto

1975 born in Alès, France | lives and works in South of France, France
www.sophiegriotto.com

*"I like to define outlines by way of
empty space; I cook the material,
the colour, and look for the attitude
that will enable me to emphasise
a personality."*

„Ich liebe es, Umrisse durch leeren Raum definieren
zu lassen. Wie ein Koch bereite ich Material und Farbe
zu und suche nach einer Haltung oder Einstellung,
mit der ich eine Persönlichkeit unterstreichen kann.“

« J'aime définir les contours par le vide, je cuisine
la matière, la couleur et recherche l'attitude qui va
me permettre de souligner une personnalité. »

↑   *Alex*, 2008, website, "Who Inspires You" for Janssen-Ortho
→   *Urban Girls*, 2008, personal work
→→ *Jalouse*, 2007, personal work

TOOLS
Pen, pencil, ink, collage,
Wacom tablet, Adobe
Photoshop, Corel Painter

CLIENTS
Swatch, Volkswagen, Clarins,
Elle (Paris), L'Express, Aéroport
de Paris, Dim, Random House

SELECTED EXHIBITIONS
_Exposition de Toiles
Digigraphiques, Galeries
Lafayette, Paris, 2008-2009

AGENT
Caroline Marechal
Paris, France
www.caroline-marechal.fr

Paris, 2008, personal work
Apesanteur, 2008, personal work
Girls, 2008, personal work
New-York Girl, 2008, Atelier Contemporain

Robert Grossman

1940 born in New York (NY), USA | lives and works in New York (NY), USA
www.robertgrossman.com

↑ *Who Eats What*, 2008, The New York Times
→ *Maverick McCain*, 2008, Rolling Stone magazine

"I think about what I'd like to see that I haven't seen before, and then I make a picture of it."

„Ich denke darüber nach, was ich gerne sehen möchte, aber noch nie vorher gesehen habe, und dann kreiere ich daraus ein Bild."

« Je pense à ce que j'aimerais voir et que je n'ai encore jamais vu, et je le dessine. »

TOOLS	CLIENTS	SELECTED AWARDS	SELECTED EXHIBITIONS
Pen, airbrush, Adobe Photoshop, painting, sculpture	Rolling Stone, The New York Times, The Nation, New York Observer	_ Academy Award Nomination 1977 _ Vargas Award 1999	_ The Arts Company, Nashville _ Society of Illustrators _ The New York Times _ The Century Association

Lisa Grue

1971 born in Kalundborg, Denmark | lives and works in Copenhagen, Denmark
www.underwerket.dk

↑ *Calendar Girls*, calendar, 2009, CWC international
→ *Lunch In The Green*, wallpaper, 2006, Wunderwear

"I define my work as very feminine and decorative. Lots of flowers, patterns, butterflies, beauty stuff, and beautiful women with a strong attitude."

„Ich definiere meine Arbeit als sehr feminin und dekorativ: viele Blumen, Muster, Schmetterlinge, schöne Dinge und schöne Frauen mit einer starken Persönlichkeit."

« Je définis mon travail comme très féminin et décoratif. Beaucoup de fleurs, de motifs, de papillons, de beaux trucs et de belles femmes avec du caractère. »

TOOLS
Pencil, watercolour, Adobe Photoshop

CLIENTS
Anna Sui, Nylon magazine, Urban Outfitters, Benefit Cosmetics

SELECTED AWARDS
_ Award from the Danish Ministry of Culture's Design Fund 2006
_ Award from Danmarks Nationalbank Fund 2008

SELECTED EXHIBITIONS
_ Dunny Show, Cph/Gallery Asbæk, 2006
_ Charlottenborg Spring exhibition, Copenhagen, 2004
_ KE, The Artists Autumn exhibition, Den Frie, Copenhagen, 2007
_ Artist in Residence, Nylon magazine, 2008
_ Danish Framing the Future Design, Danish Design Center, 2005

AGENT
CWC International
New York, USA
www.cwc-i.com

CWC
Tokyo, Japan
www.cwctokyo.com

Santiago Guerrero

1969 born in Córdoba, Argentina | lives and works in Córdoba, Argentina
www.santiagoguerrero.com.ar

"I'm mainly interested in a kind of ridiculous, ironic, and retro tribute to science fiction. A mix between comics and graphic design."

„Mich interessiert vor allem eine Art alberner und ironischer Retro-Tribut an Science Fiction – eine Mischung aus Comics und Grafikdesign."

« Ma principale ambition est de rendre une sorte d'hommage grotesque, ironique et rétro à la science fiction. A mi-chemin entre la bande dessinée et le design graphique. »

↑   *Babylon Diciembre 08*, poster, 2008, Casa Babylon Club
→   *Babylon Abril 08*, poster, 2008, Casa Babylon Club
→→ *Babylon Noviembre 07*, poster, 2008, Casa Babylon Club

TOOLS
Pen, pencil, paintbrush, markers, paper, digital camera, Adobe Illustrator

CLIENTS
Centro Cultural España-Córdoba, Casa Babylon Club, Revista Ñ (Diario Clarín)

Jon Han

1981 born in San Pedro (CA), USA | lives and works in Los Angeles (CA), USA
www.jon-han.com

↑   *Story in Story*, 2008, Los Angeles Times Book Review. Art Director: Carol Kaufman
→   *The Bull*, 2008, The New York Times Op/Ed. Art Director: Kim Bost
→→   *Newer*, 2008, The Deal. Art Director: Larry Gendron

"A different vintage. Mixing the common with the uncommon, and with what is understood within the abstract."

„Eine ganz andere Liga – das Mischen von Bekanntem mit dem Unbekannten, Unüblichen und damit, was man im Abstrakten begreifen kann."

« Un millésime à part. Mêlant l'ordinaire à l'insolite, et le compréhensible à l'abstrait. »

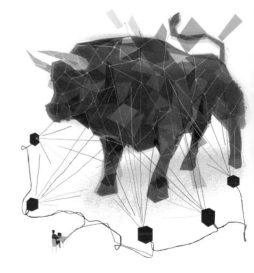

TOOLS
Ink, paint, graphite, sticks, Adobe Photoshop, screens, paper, gouache, camera, words, glue, rulers

CLIENTS
The New Yorker, The New York Times, Los Angeles Times, BusinessWeek, Cramer-Krasselt, Runner's World, VSA Partners, HHMI, GOOD magazine, Globe and Mail, The New York Sun, National Television

SELECTED AWARDS
_ Communication Arts magazine
_ American Illustration
_ Print magazine
_ Society of Illustrators New York
_ CMYK Conference

SELECTED EXHIBITIONS
_ The Illustrated Letter, Gallery Seven (The New York Times), New York
_ SUKU, Abacot Gallery
_ Imaginative Landscapes, Nucleus Gallery
_ Supernal, Compound Gallery

Sun Block, 2008, Bulletin of the Atomic Scientists. Art Director: Joy Olivia Miller

↘ *You Make It, We Make It*, 2008, The magazine Group, Independent School magazine. Art Director: Glenn Pierce

↓ *Fall Unfolds*, Fall Preview cover art, 2008, The New York Sun. Art Director: Kristofer Porter

Jonny Hannah

1971 born in Dunfermline, UK | lives and works in Southampton, UK

↑ *Mingus Says...*, 2008, personal work
→ *Shakespeare*, 2007, Telegraph Newspapers, Seven magazine
→→ *Gershwin*, 2007, The New York Times Book Review

"I love getting my hands dirty in the print room. I love drawing typography, a wee bit wobbly. I try and do something a wee bit different every time."

„Ich liebe es, mir im Druckraum die Hände schmutzig zu machen. Ich zeichne liebend gerne Typografie … auch ein bisschen wackelig. Ich versuche, Dinge jedes Mal ein wenig anders zu machen."

« J'adore me salir les mains dans le print-room. J'adore dessiner de la typographie, un tantinet bancale. J'essaie et je fais quelque chose d'un peu différent chaque fois. »

TOOLS

Ink, brushes, gouache, acrylic, screenprinting, lino-cuts, printing presses, Adobe Photoshop, scanner

CLIENTS

Folio Society, RIBA, Penguin, Telegraph Newspaper, English National Opera, Miramax, New York Times, Vogue, Sony, Amnesty International, GQ, Atlantic Records, Camel, Los Angeles Times.

SELECTED AWARDS

_ V&A Illustration Awards 2005
_ BAFTA 2000

SELECTED EXHIBITIONS

_ St. Judes in the City, Bankside Gallery, London, 2009
_ Hot Dogs & Rocket Fuel, solo exhibition, Castor & Pollux, Brighton, 2007
_ Works from the Cakes & Ale Press solo exhibition, Chelsea & Westminsteer Hospital, 2005
_ Notes from The Captain, solo exhibition, Brighton Fishing Museum, 2001
_ Horse Opera solo exhibition, Groucho Club, London, 1999

AGENT

Heart
London, UK
www.heartagency.com

Heart USA
New York, USA
www.heartagency.com

Tony Healey

1959 born in Wales, UK | lives and works in London, UK
www.th-illustration.co.uk

↑　*BB King*, exhibition, 2005, personal work
→　*Miles Davis*, exhibition, 2005, personal work
→→ *Ray Charles*, exhibition, 2005, personal work

*"There is a great tradition of pen and ink illustration here in the UK.
I would like to think that my work follows in the footsteps of that tradition,
albeit that nowadays the pen is made by Wacom and there is no ink, only pixels."*

*„Hier in Großbritannien gibt es eine großartige Tradition der Illustration mit Stift und Tusche.
Ich stelle mir gerne vor, dass ich mit meiner Arbeit in die Fußstapfen dieser Tradition trete,
obwohl der Stift heutzutage von Wacom gemacht wird und es keine Tusche gibt, sondern nur noch Pixel."*

*« Ici, au Royaume Uni, il y a une longue tradition d'illustration à la plume et à l'encre. J'aime penser que mon travail
en suit les traces, même si la plume est aujourd'hui fabriquée par Wacom et s'il n'y pas d'encre, seulement des pixels. »*

TOOLS
Pencil, ink, watercolour,
digital media

CLIENTS
BBC, Barclays Bank, Guinness,
Penguin Books, Esquire,
Vodafone, The Daily Telegraph,
The Observer, Financial Times

SELECTED EXHIBITIONS
_ Garrick Milne Prize,
Christie's, London, 2005
_ Singer Friedlander (Sunday
Times Watercolour exhibition),
Mall Galleries, London, 2006
_ Art About Face, Shrewsbury
Cartoon Festival, UK, 2008
_ Images/The Best of British
Contemporary Illustration
(Aoi), London College of
Communication, London,
2003-2005, 2008

AGENT
Anna Goodson Management
Montreal, Canada
www.agoodson.com

David Heatley

1974 born in Ridgewood (NJ), USA | lives and works in Jackson Heights (NY), USA
www.davidheatley.com

← *Anthony Flew*, 2008, The New York Times Book Review
→ *The Comic Book Nightmare*, 2006, Nickelodeon magazine
↓ *Shopping Cart*, magazine cover, 2008, First Story

"I'm a writer, artist, cartoonist, musician, and illustrator, probably in that order. But learning illustration taught me everything else."

„Ich bin Schriftsteller, Künstler, Cartoonist, Musiker und Illustrator – wahrscheinlich auch in dieser Reihenfolge. Doch durch die Illustrationen habe ich auch alles andere gelernt."

« Je suis écrivain, artiste, bédéiste, musicien et illustrateur, dans cet ordre, probablement. Mais avoir appris l'illustration m'a enseigné tout le reste. »

TOOLS
Ink, pen, brush on bristol, Adobe Photoshop

CLIENTS
The New Yorker, The New York Times, Nickelodeon magazine, Random House, WonderSound Records, Granta, McSweeney's, Fantagraphics Books, Houghton Mifflin

SELECTED AWARDS
_NYFA Fellowship for Fiction 2008

SELECTED EXHIBITIONS
_The Cartoonist's Eye, A+D Gallery of Columbia College, Chicago, 2005
_Contemporary Literary Comics: Selections from McSweeney's #13, Museum of Cartoon Art, San Francisco, 2005

_Comix Chicago, Hyde Park Art Center, Chicago, 2003
_The New Graphics Revival (co-curated and showed work at this gallery show), Butcher Shop, Chicago, 2002
_Multiples 4, NFA Space, Chicago, 2000

AGENT
McCormick & Williams
New York, USA
www.mccormickwilliams.com

Julia Sonmi Heglund

1983 born in Memphis (TN), USA | lives and works in Madison (WI), USA
www.sonmisonmi.com

"I enjoy childlike styles and whimsical worlds. Hard, angular edges that clash with organic forms."

„Mir machen kindliche Stile und verrückte Welten viel Spaß – harte, eckige Kanten, die auf organische Formen treffen."

« J'aime les styles enfantins et les mondes fantasques. Les contours angulaires, durs, qui tranchent sur les formes organiques. »

↑ *Untitled*, tattoo, 2006
→ *Consumption*, T-shirt, 2008, Threadless.com
→→ *Daydream*, T-shirt, 2008, Design By Humans

TOOLS
Micron pen, paper, markers, watercolours, mechanical pencil, Wacom tablet, Adobe Photoshop

CLIENTS
Threadless.com, Design by Humans, Timbuk2, Shirt.woot, Funkrush, Naked & Angry

SELECTED AWARDS
_Threadless Bestee Awards 2007

SELECTED EXHIBITIONS
_New Work by Audrey Kawasaki & Friends, The Drawing Room, Thinkspace Gallery, Los Angeles, USA

↑ *Believe It*, T-shirt, 2008, Threadless.com
↗ *Untitled*, T-shirt, 2007, Heavy Rotation Tees
→ *Fox and Hare*, T-shirt, 2007, Threadless.com

Regina Heinlein

1980 born in Nürnberg, Germany | lives and works in Berlin, Germany, and London, UK
www.foersterstochter.de

← *Cosmic Relations III*, 2008, personal wor[k]
→ *Womentree 01*, T-shirt, 2008, Anna Sui
↓ *Womentree 02*, 2008, personal work

"When I'm not drawing, I'm happy. When I'm drawing, there is no more 'I.'"

*„Wenn ich nicht zeichne, bin ich glücklich.
Wenn ich zeichne, bin ,ich' nicht mehr vorhanden."*

*« Quand je ne dessine pas, je suis heureuse.
Quand je dessine, il n'y a plus de ‹je›. »*

TOOLS
Ink pen, gouache, acrylic
paint, paper, scanner,
Adobe Photoshop

CLIENTS
Anna Sui, BR, Hermes,
Loewe, BYM

SELECTED EXHIBITIONS
_ Ogilvy & Mather
Headquarters, New York, 2008
_ Gallery Hanahou, New York
_ Studio Banana, Madrid
_ Wallstreet One Gallery, Berlin

AGENT
CWC International
New York, USA
www.cwc-i.com

CWC
Tokyo, Japan
www.cwctokyo.com

Ryan Heshka

1970 born in Brandon (MB), Canada | lives and works in Sherman Oaks (CA), USA
www.ryanheshka.com

← *BLAB! #18 feature splash*, 2007, BLAB!/Fantagraphics
Art Director: Monte Beauchamp
→ *Electric Eye vs. Thermo-Woman*, 2007, personal work,
Roq La Rue Gallery, Seattle
↓ *Mad Science*, student dayplanner cover, 2007, University of Guelph

"In my work, I try to draw on the viewer's 'pop culture subconscious' by creating images that are both familiar yet new to the viewer."

„In meiner Arbeit beziehe ich mich auf das von ‚Popkultur geprägte Unterbewusstsein' des Betrachters, indem ich Bilder schaffe, die für ihn sowohl vertraut als auch neu und ungewohnt sind."

« Dans mon travail, j'essaie de viser le ‹ subconscient de culture populaire › que le spectateur a en lui, en créant des images qui lui soient à la fois familières et nouvelles. »

TOOLS
Gouache, acrylic, mixed media

CLIENTS
Henry Holt, Little Brown,
Vanity Fair, Esquire, Blab!,
The New York Times,
The Wall Street Journal,
Smart Money, Travel + Leisure,
Runner's World, AARP

SELECTED AWARDS
_ Society of Illustrators 49
_ American Illustration 24
_ Communication Arts
magazine
_ Western magazine Awards
2003

SELECTED EXHIBITIONS
_ Society of Illustrators 49,
Group show
_ BLAB! Show, 2008
_ Roq La Rue Anniversary
Show, 2008

AGENT
Kate Larkworthy Artist
Representation
New York, USA
www.larkworthy.com

Tiago Hoisel

1984 born in Salvador, Bahia, Brazil | lives and works in São Paulo, Brazil
http://hoisel.zip.net

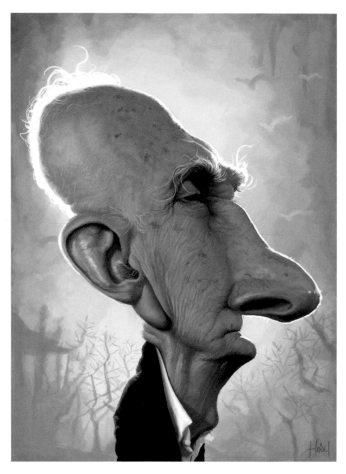

"To illustrate is more than simply to produce an image. It's to enhance my perception of the world in all its complexity at every moment."

„Beim Illustrieren geht es um mehr als einfach nur ein Bild zu erschaffen. Es geht darum, meine Wahrnehmung der Welt in ihrer Komplexität in jedem einzelnen Moment zu erweitern."

« Illustrer est davantage que produire une image. C'est accroître ma perception du monde dans toute sa complexité, à chaque instant. »

↑   *Ariano Suassuna*, 2008, personal work
→   *Morgan Freeman*, 2008, personal work
→→ *Axl Rose Rooster*, 2008, Leo Burnett Brazil
    Art Director: J.R. D'Elboux

TOOLS
Adobe Photoshop,
Wacom tablet

CLIENTS
Leo Burnett Brazil, Leo Burnett Lebanon, DM9DDB, ZMais, MDesign, Veja magazine, Playboy magazine, Super Interessante magazine

SELECTED AWARDS
_ 22nd/23rd International Humor Contest from Piauí
_ Academic Humor Contest from Piracicaba 2005/2007
_ Festival of Honorable Mention for Cartoonists, Brazil 2007

SELECTED EXHIBITIONS
_ Porto Cartoon, Portugal, 2008
_ Piracicaba International Humor Exhibition, Brazil, 2007–2008
_ 8th Tehran International Cartoon Biennial, Iran, 2007
_ Porto Alegre International Salon of Drawing for Press, Brazil, 2005

Seonna Hong

1973 born in Los Angeles (CA), USA | lives and works in Los Angeles (CA), USA
www.seonnahong.com

↑   *Mix Tape*, 2007, personal work
→   *If A Tree Falls In The Forest*, 2007, personal work

"I'd define my work as melancholic narratives."

„Ich würde meine Arbeit als melancholische Erzählungen definieren."

« Je définirais ce que je fais comme des récits mélancoliques. »

TOOLS
Acrylic, paper, charcoal on canvas, wood

CLIENTS
Takashi Murakami, François Pinault

SELECTED AWARDS
_ Joan Mitchell Foundation Grant Recipient
_ Emmy Award

SELECTED EXHIBITIONS
_ Viscery Loves Company, Kaikai Kiki Gallery, Tokyo, 2008
_ Our Endless Numbered Days, Oliver Kamm Gallery, New York, 2007
_ People in the City, Six Space Gallery, Los Angeles, 2005
_ Knoxville Museum Retrospective, Knoxville, 2006

↑   *Self Defeating*, 2006, personal work
→   *I Am Not Permanent*, 2006, personal work
←   *Constructing The Deconstruction*, 2008, personal work

Brian Hubble

1978 born in Hampton (VA), USA | lives and works in Brooklyn (NY), USA
www.levycreative.com

"I compose photo-collage illustrations by means of screen-printing, photo-transferring, scratching, and melting images on to canvas and glass."

„Ich stelle Illustrationen als Fotocollagen zusammen, indem ich Bilder als Serigrafien oder Fotos transferiere oder Bilder in Leinwand und Glas kratze und schmelze."

« Je compose des illustrations par photocollage, à l'aide de la sérigraphie, du transfert de photo, des effets de scratching, de la fusion des images sur toile et verre. »

↑   *Children at Risk Series*, 2006, The American School Board Journal
→   *Fighting the System from the Inside and Outside*, 2006, Notre Dame magazine
→→ *Increasing Tornadoes in Suburban US*, 2008, Our State magazine

TOOLS
Photo-transfers, cray-pas, graphite, oil sticks, acrylic, clear tape, glass

CLIENTS
New York Times, American Lawyer, New York Press, Atlanta, The Atlantic, Harper's, Avenue, Nylon magazine, San Francisco Chronicle, Columbia Journal Review, NYU School of Law, Golf World

SELECTED AWARDS
_ The Addy Award
_ The Illustration Academy Scholarship
_ The Commonwealth Award

SELECTED EXHIBITIONS
_ Digital Z-Print Exhibition, Yes Gallery, New York, 2009
_ Inaugural Exhibition, Art Raw Gallery, New York, 2009
_ Midnite Snacks: A Traveling Group Exhibition (curator), 2009
_ Variation on a Theme, Rabbithole Gallery, New York , 2008

AGENT
Levy Creative Management New York, USA
www.levycreative.com

Rian Hughes

1963 born in London, UK | lives and works in London, UK
www.rianhughes.com

"My work sits squarely between design and illustration. For me the type is as much an integral part of the image-making process as the image itself."

„Meine Arbeiten stehen direkt zwischen Design und Illustration. Für mich ist die Ausführung ein ebenso integraler Bestandteil des Vorgangs, ein Bild herzustellen, wie das Bild selbst."

« Mon travail se situe franchement entre le design et l'illustration. Pour moi, le caractère fait partie intégrante de la fabrication de l'image, au même titre que l'image elle-même. »

↑ *Louche*, "Crumble Crackle Burn" book, 2007,
Von Glitschka/HOW Books
→ *Marlowe*, 2007, Knockabout
→→ *Really and Truly*, 2007, Knockabout

TOOLS
Adobe Illustrator, Adobe Photoshop, brush and ink, pencil

CLIENTS
Virgin Airlines, MTV, Mother, St. Lukes, McCann Eriksson, JWT, DC Comics, The Face, Cosmopolitan, Maxim, BBC, The Guardian, Cartoon Network, Marvel Comics, Penguin Books, Hasbro

SELECTED AWARDS
_ New York Art Directors Club 79th Annual Awards
_ AP&PB Best Use of Print 1996
_ BDA International 1996 (Broadcasting Design Awards)
_ Campaign Press Advertising Awards 1995

SELECTED EXHIBITIONS
_ Toybox solo exhibition, Conningsby Gallery, London, 2003
_ Powerhouse, Horse Guards Parade, London, 1999
_ Café Casbar solo exhibition, Smith's Gallery, Covent Garden, London, 1990

Interact Creative

2006 founded in Porto, Portugal | is Benedita Feijó & Michael Andersen
www.interactcreative.com

"We are always trying to come up with new approaches and ideas, both work-wise and personally, creating unique stuff, having fun and believing in it."

„Wir versuchen stets, uns neue Ansätze und Ideen einfallen zu lassen, sowohl was die Arbeitsweise angeht als auch für uns persönlich, um einzigartige Sachen zu schaffen, um Spaß zu haben und damit wir von der Arbeit überzeugt sind."

« Dans le travail comme dans la vie, nous essayons toujours de proposer de nouvelles approches et de nouvelles idées, en créant des trucs uniques, en nous éclatant et en y croyant. »

↑   *Bird Wallpaper*, custom wallpaper, 2006, Teka
→   *Brain*, website, 2009, Young & Rubicam
→→ *Dif*, 2008, Dif magazine

TOOLS
Adobe Photoshop, Adobe Illustrator, digital camera

CLIENTS
Absolut, Compal, Teka, Rojo , J.B. Whisky, Soares da Costa, Super Bock

SELECTED AWARDS
_ Eurobest 2006
_ Innovative Advertising Awards (NYF)
_ Epica 2006
_ Webby Awards
_ Scandinavian Advertising Awards 2006

SELECTED EXHIBITIONS
_ Rojo Out 3, Barcelona, 2009
_ Super Bock, Porto/Lisbon/Faro, 2008
_ Vilar Gallery, Porto, 2006
_ Ipanema Gallery, 2005
_ Rivoli Theater, 2004

Josie Jammet

1970 born in London, UK | lives and works in London, UK

← *The Who*, 2004, Rolling Stone magazine
→ *Robbie Williams*, 2008, The Guardian Weekend magazine
↓ *Hardip Singh*, annual report, 2006, Channel 4, UK

"My work examines and reinterprets photographic references to create new and previously unseen responses to classic images."

„In meiner Arbeit untersuche ich fotografische Verweise und interpretiere sie neu, damit ich neue und bisher ungesehene Antworten auf klassische Bilder schaffe."

« Mon travail consiste à examiner et réinterpréter des références photographiques afin de créer des réponses nouvelles et inédites aux images classiques. »

TOOLS
Acrylic paint on canvas

CLIENTS
Rolling Stone, Sydney Opera House, The Guardian, Channel 4, Nike, Esquire, Vanity Fair, Random House, Penguin USA, New Scientist, Time Out, New York magazine, Vibe, American Express

SELECTED EXHIBITIONS
_ It Feels Like I Know You, Space Gallery, London, 2004
_ Heart Group Show, Art Directors Club, New York, 2003

AGENT
Heart
London, UK
www.heartagency.com

Heart USA
New York, USA
www.heartagency.com

Mireia Juárez Noriega

1970 born in Mexico City, Mexico | lives and works in Madrid, Spain

"It is not what is seen in the illustration, it is the unseen context of the illustration which makes the brain generate a story from first seeing the image."

„Es geht nicht darum, was man in der Illustration selbst sieht, sondern um ihren unsichtbaren Kontext, durch den das Gehirn vom ersten Anblick des Bildes an eine Geschichte generiert."

« C'est le contexte invisible de l'illustration, et non ce qu'on en voit, qui suscite une histoire dans le cerveau lorsqu'on découvre l'image. »

← *Like This?*, 2008, Frame
→ *Untitled*, 2008, Frame

TOOLS
Freehand, Adobe Photoshop

CLIENTS
Thoren Entertainment, FFI International

AGENT
Smart Magna
Athens, Greece
www.smartmagna.com

David Juniper

1946 born in London, UK | lives and works in Uplyme, UK
www.folioart.co.uk

"Inspired by the Art Deco period and with a personal retro take. Design-led work, so that typography plays a large part in each image."

„Inspirationen aus dem Art Déco, interpretiert mit einem ganz persönlichen Retro-Touch. Das Design führt die Arbeiten, damit die Typografie auf jedem Bild eine große Rolle spielt."

« Inspiré par la période Art Déco, avec un penchant personnel pour le rétro. Travail à tendance design, où la typographie joue donc un rôle majeur dans chaque image. »

↑ *West Indies*, 2008, Bentley Publishing USA
→ *Daytona Beach*, 2008, Bentley Publishing USA
→→ *Marlin Miami Beach*, 2007, self-promotion

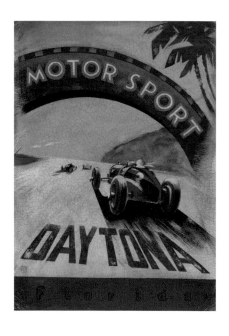

TOOLS
Acrylic, gouache on board, digital additions

CLIENTS
Ogilvy, Y&R, TBWA, Leo Burnett, Saatchi & Saatchi, VW, Marks & Spencer, Harper Collins, Random House, Penguin Books, Daily Telegraph, The Guardian, The Times, Evening Standard

SELECTED AWARDS
_D&AD Illustration Awards
_Grammy Award

SELECTED EXHIBITIONS
_European Illustration
_AOI Illustration Exhibitions

AGENT
Folio
London, UK
www.folioart.co.uk

Kako

1975 born in São Paulo, Brazil | lives and works in São Paulo, Brazil
www.kakofonia.com

"Keep mind, eyes, and hands busy."

„Halte stets den Geist, die Augen und die Hände beschäftigt."

« Toujours avoir l'esprit, les yeux et les mains occupés. »

↑   *Samurai*, 2008, Editora Abril, Grandes Guerras magazine
→   *Ohimesama*, book, 2007, Catalogue
→→ *O Japão Daqui*, poster and postcard, 2008, Editora Abril

TOOLS
Adobe Illustrator, Adobe Photoshop

CLIENTS
McCann Erickson, Saatchi & Saatchi, BBDO, TBWA, AOL, Nokia, Coca-Cola, GM, Diesel, MTV, Editora Abril, Scholastic, Playboy, Rolling Stone, Popular Mechanics, Texas Monthly, DC/Vertigo Comics

SELECTED AWARDS
_ Cannes Lions Festival 2008
_ El Ojo de Iberoamerica 2008
_ Prêmio HQ MIX 2007

SELECTED EXHIBITIONS
_ 51ˢᵗ Society of Illustrators Annual Exhibition, New York, 2009
_ Creative Art Session, Kawasaki, Japan, 2008
_ Desenhos, Galeria Deco, São Paulo, 2008

_ WIWP, Now Showing, London/Barcelona, 2008
_ Katalogue XXL, London, 2007

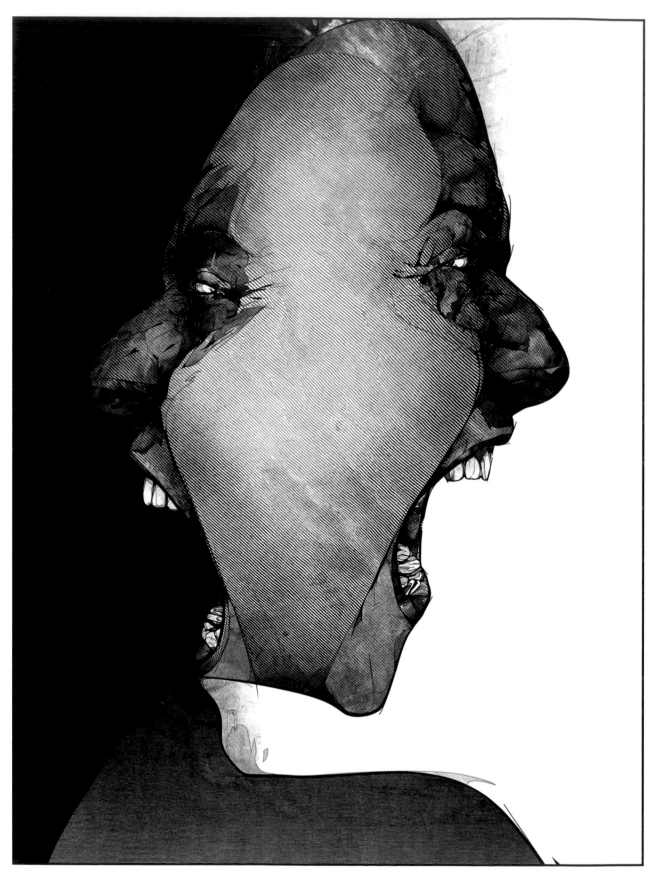

238

↑   *The Trial*, 2008, Almap BBDO
←   *White Fang*, book, 2008, Editora Scipione
←← *Conflict*, poster, 2008, Itaú Cultural

Jörn Kaspuhl

1980 born in Stade, Germany | lives and works in Hamburg, Germany
www.kaspuhl.com

"An organic combination of strong line-drawings and hatching paired with a graphic colour palette."

„Eine organische Kombination von kräftigen Linienzeichnungen und Schraffierungen, gepaart mit einer grafischen Farbpalette."

« Une combinaison organique de robustes dessins au trait et de hachures, associés à une palette graphique de couleurs. »

↑   *Alain Souchon*, 2009, GQ France. Art Director: Paul Chemetoff
→   *Mouflon*, 2009, DGPH, contribution for "The Ark Book Project"
→→ *Modern Sex*, 2008, The Independent magazine. Art Director: Stephen Petch

---

TOOLS
Pen, ink, Adobe Photoshop

CLIENTS
Monocle, The Independent, Fast Company, Nylon magazine, Wired, GQ, Die Zeit, Zeit Magazin, Der Spiegel, SZ Magazin, NZZ am Sonntag, Human Empire, YCN, Jung von Matt, Factor Design

SELECTED EXHIBITIONS
_Illustrative, Zurich, 2008

AGENT
Dutch Uncle
London, UK
www.dutchuncle.co.uk

Ian Kim

1982 born in Harbor City (CA), USA | lives and works in Los Angeles (CA), USA
www.iankim.net

← *Exit Ghost*, 2007, The Village Voice newspaper
Art Director: LD Beghtol
→ *A Corpse in the Koryo*, 2007, KoreAm Journal magazine
Art Director: Corina Knoll
↓ *Exiles on Main Street*, 2007, KoreAm Journal magazine
Art Director: Corina Knoll

*"My artwork is the product of years
of drawing practice and a desire to broaden
my understanding of the world."*

*„Meine Kunst ist das Produkt jahrelanger zeichnerischer Übung
und dem tiefen Wunsch, die Welt tiefer und weiter zu verstehen."*

*« Mes illustrations sont le fruit d'années de pratique
et de mon désir d'étendre ma compréhension du monde. »*

TOOLS
Graphite, coloured pencils,
acrylic, paper, Adobe
Photoshop, Adobe Illustrator,
Wacom tablet

CLIENTS
City Pages, ColorLines,
Education Week, Hyphen,
Imaginary Forces, KoreAm
Journal, Motion Theory,
Picture Mill, Popular
Mechanics, Prologue, Runner's
World, Village Voice, Transistor
Studios

SELECTED AWARDS
_ The Society of Illustrators
Los Angeles

SELECTED EXHIBITIONS
_ My Life in Progress,
solo show, Asian Pacific
American Studies Gallery,
New York, 2004

Jonathan Klassen

1981 born in Winnipeg, Manitoba, Canada | lives and works in Los Angeles (CA), USA
www.burstofbeaden.com

↑ *Castles*, 2007, personal work
↓ *Beach House*, 2008, personal work
→ *Waterfall*, 2008, personal work

"I like telling stories to myself."

„Ich erzähle mir gerne selbst Geschichten."

« J'aime bien me raconter des histoires. »

TOOLS
Watercolour, papers, scanner,
Adobe Photoshop

CLIENTS
Dreamworks, Laika Inc.,
Harper Collins, Simon &
Schuster, The Ebeling Group

SELECTED EXHIBITIONS
_ Great Great Grand Show,
Gallery Nucleus
_ Ottawa International Film
Festival
_ Pictoplasma
_ New York Childrens Film
Festival
_ Fotokino

AGENT
Steven Malk
San Diego, USA
www.writershouse.com

Koa

1975 born in Nantes, France | lives and works in Lille, France
www.koadzn.com

"*A universe of happy and colourful yet oppressive chaos where monsters are masters and humans are slaves. A universe full of bearded women, dwarf hip-hop masters, ridiculous ghosts, strange dogs…*"

„*Ein ganzes Universum voller Chaos, glücklich und farbenfroh, aber doch bedrückend, wo Monster die Herren sind und Menschen die Sklaven. Ein Universum voller bärtiger Frauen, zwergenhafter Hip-Hop-Meister, lächerlicher Geister, bizarrer Hunde …*"

« *Un univers de chaos radieux et coloré, et pourtant oppressant, où les monstres sont les maîtres et les hommes leurs esclaves. Un univers tout plein de femmes à barbe, de nains champions de hip-hop, de fantômes grotesques, d'étranges chiens… »*

← *Dog of Acid*, 2008, L issue
→ *Kid Oignon*, 2008, Artoyz

TOOLS
Pencil, paper, canvas, paint, ink, Adobe Photoshop, Wacom tablet

CLIENTS
British Gas, Nickelodeon, Publicis, TBWA, EuroRSCG, Burton, XBox, Salamon Snowboards, 3D Eye Design

SELECTED EXHIBITIONS
_ Untitled, L Issue, Paris
_ War of Monsters, Lazy Dog
_ La Collective, Galerie LJ Beaubourg, Paris
_ Forward, Galerie LJ Beaubourg, Paris
_ Solo exhibition, Extrabold Gallery, Luxembourg

AGENT
Lezilus
Paris, France
www.lezilus.com

Stem Agency
London, UK
www.stemagency.com

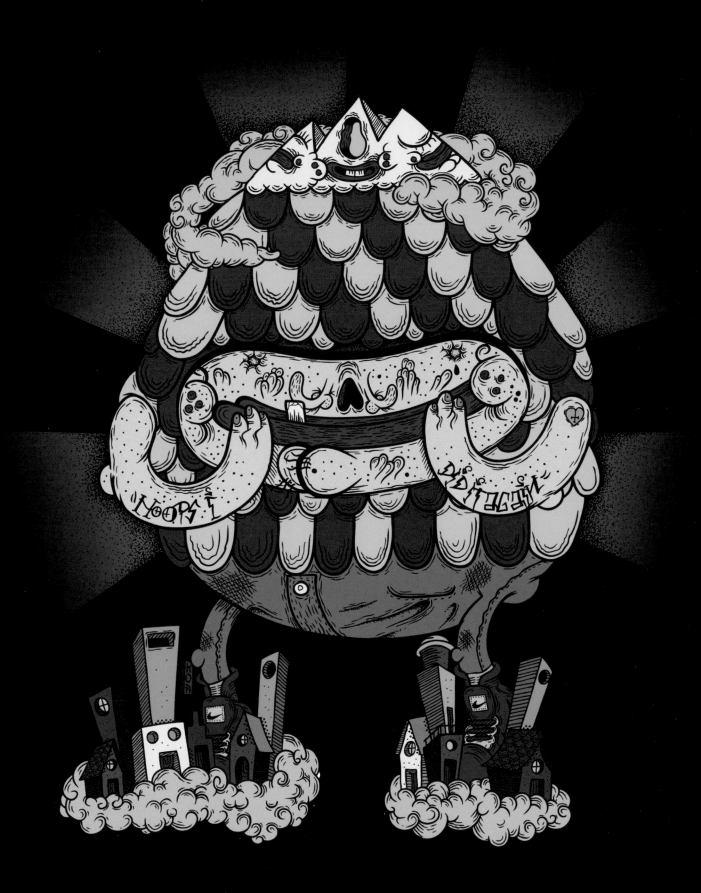

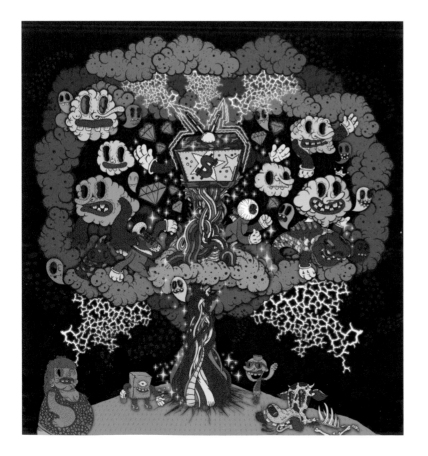

↑ *5 Boro*, skateboard design, 2009, 5 Boro, design done with Dekore
← *Jack and the Seed of Life*, poster, 2008, Piranha Bar
→ *Kid Dream*, 2008, Nickelodeon/Mainframe

Viktor Koen

1967 born in Thessaloniki, Greece | lives and works in New York (NY), USA
www.viktorkoen.com

← *Nutrition Man*, 2005, Men's Journal
Art Director: David Matt
→ *Global Warning*, 2006, Baseline
International Typographics magazine
Art Director: Steve Heller
↓ *No Easy Fix*, 2008, Bloomberg
Art Director: Cody Schneider

"I am visually addicted to industrial surfaces, machines, and rust, so these are the environments in which my creatures and characters feel comfortable."

„Ich bin visuell regelrecht süchtig nach industriellen Oberflächen, Maschinen und Rost. Darum ist das die Umgebung, in der meine Kreaturen und Figuren sich wohl fühlen."

« Je suis accroc aux zones industrielles, aux machines, à la rouille, c'est donc dans ce genre de décors que mes créatures et mes personnages se sentent à l'aise. »

TOOLS
Adobe Photoshop, digital photography

CLIENTS
The New York Times, Time magazine, Newsweek, Esquire, Penguin Putnam, Random House, Doubleday, Harper Collins, Rizzoli, Houghton Mifflin, National Geographic, Rolling Stone, Wired, Sports Illustrated, Reader's Digest

SELECTED AWARDS
_ Purchase Awards, Arkansas Art Center 2008
_ Folio Awards 2005
_ Bethesda International Photography Competition 2004
_ Digital Hall of Fame, Sweden 2003
_ Kounio/Hasselblad Award, Greece 2001

SELECTED EXHIBITIONS
_ Art District 798, Beijing, 2008
_ Benaki Museum, Athens, 2006
_ National Museum, Canberra, 2006
_ Kiyosato Museum of Photographic Arts, Japan, 2004
_ Macedonian Museum of Contemporary Art, Thessaloniki, Greece, 2001

Ilana Kohn

1981 born in Arlington (VA), USA | lives and works in Brooklyn (NY), USA
www.ilanakohn.com

← *Untitled 03*, 2008, personal work
→ *Cell Break*, newspaper cover, 2008, Seattle Weekly
  Art Director: Jane Sherman
↓ *Untitled 01*, 2008, personal work

*"I see my work as being a repeated challenge
to impose a little of myself successfully on to new
and exciting subject matter time and time again."*

*„Ich betrachte meine Arbeit als wiederholte Herausforderung, einem neuen und
spannenden Thema immer wieder erfolgreich ein Stück meiner selbst aufzudrücken."*

*« Je considère mon travail comme un défi répété de me colleter victorieusement,
encore et encore, avec des sujets nouveaux et exaltants. »*

TOOLS
Acrylic, collage,
Adobe Photoshop

CLIENTS
The New York Times, HOW,
American Medical News,
The Deal, The Advovate,
The Washington City Paper,
LA Weekly, The Stranger,
Seattle Weekly, Jazziz,
Ohio magazine

SELECTED EXHIBITIONS
_ Downright, PEP Gallery,
New York, 2007
_ The First Ever LA Weekly
Biennial, Track 16 Gallery,
Los Angeles, 2005
_ Society of Illustrators Student
Exhibition, Society of
Illustrators, New York, 2004

← *Milwaukee Wine Bars*, 2008, My Midwest magazine
  Art Director: Shane Luitjens
→ *The Writer Rockstar*, 2008, Las Vegas City Life
  Art Director: Maureen Adamo
↓ *Contributor Portraits*, 2006, HOW magazine
  Art Director: Susan Smith

Signý Kolbeinsdóttir

1978 born in Reykjavik, Iceland | lives and works in Reykjavik, Iceland
www.signy.net

"My work covers a spectrum from soft Japanese manga, and colourful fairy-tales, to picturesque surreal dreams and nightmares."

„Meine Arbeiten erstrecken sich in einem Spektrum von sanften japanischen Mangas und farbenprächtige Märchen bis hin zu malerischen surrealen Träumen und Alpträumen."

« Mon travail couvre un spectre allant du manga japonais soft au conte de fées haut en couleurs, en passant par les cauchemars et les rêves surréalistes pittoresques. »

↑   *Buddha*, postcard and book cover, 2008, personal work
→   *Xmas in Hong Kong*, Christmas card, 2007, Landsbanki Hong Kong
→→ *Tokyo Tako*, postcard and book cover, 2007, personal work

---

TOOLS
Adobe Illustrator, Adobe Photoshop, Wacom tablet

CLIENTS
Epal, Nikita Clothing, Penninn Eymundsson, Landsbankinn, Vis, Naked Ape, Birkiland, Kisan

SELECTED EXHIBITIONS
_ Home and Design, Laugardalsholl Hall, Reykjavik, 2007
_ Design Days, Reykjavik, 2005

Ronald Kurniawan

1979 born in Jakarta, Indonesia | lives and works in Los Angeles (CA), USA
http://ronaldkurniawan.com

↑   *CarSick*, 2008, Roq La Rue Gallery
→   *Anxiety*, 2008, The New York Times

"Inspired by ideograms, syllables, letter-forms, beasts, and heroic landscapes."

„Inspiration durch Ideogramme, Silben, Buchstabenformen, wilde Tieren und heroische Landschaften."

« Inspiré par les idéogrammes, les syllabaires, les dessins de lettres, les bêtes et les paysages héroïques. »

TOOLS
Graphite, watercolour paper, ink, parchment paper, watercolour, dyes, acrylic, brushes, computer, Wacom tablet, cintiq, iPhone

CLIENTS
Dreamworks, Disney, Sony, Mattel, HP, Saatchi, W+K, TBWA, McCann Erickson, Mother, Passion Pictures, MTV, Entertainment Weekly, LA Weekly, The New York Times, LA Times, Bloomsbury, Harvard, Plansponsor, Wired

SELECTED EXHIBITIONS
_ Summer Solstice Painting, Los Angeles County Museum of Art
_ Giant Baboon Painting, Roq la Rue Gallery
_ The Drawing Club

AGENT
Sam Summerskill
London, UK
www.debutart.com

↑ *Treasure Hunt*, 2007, LA Weekly newspaper

↑   *Hidden in Plain Sight*, 2008, Plansponsor magazine

↑ *B Wary*, 2006, Plansponsor magazine
← *Thinking Brain*, 2008, Mens Health Germany magazine
↓ *Summer Solstice*, 2007, LACMA

Julien Langendorff

1982 born in Paris, France | lives and works in Paris, France
www.julienlangendorff.com

↑   *Untitled*, album artwork, 2006, Jordan
→   *Untitled*, 2008, Talkie Walkie, self-promotion
→→ *Untitled*, 2008, Vice magazine

"I just try to create images that belong to peculiar visions of mine. A pre-Raphaelite painter writing his diary drunk at night in the company of Black Sabbath."

„Ich versuche einfach, Bilder zu schaffen, die zu meinen eigenartigen Visionen passen – wie ein präraffaelitischer Maler, der nachts betrunken in sein Tagebuch schreibt und dazu Black Sabbath hört."

« Je m'efforce juste de reproduire des images qui peuplent mes visions personnelles. Un peintre préraphaélite qui écrirait son journal nuitamment, ivre, en compagnie de Black Sabbath. »

TOOLS
Pen, magic markers, papercuts

CLIENTS
Citizen K magazine, Playboy magazine, Vice magazine, Jalouse magazine, Agnès B., San Pellegrino, Andrea Crews, Fooding, Zombie Zombie

SELECTED EXHIBITIONS
_ Solar Disturbance, Fat Galerie, Paris, 2009
_ Playlist, Galerie Patricia Dorfmann, Paris, 2008
_ Where is it slowly going? (collaborative show with David-Ivar Herman Dune), Cinders Gallery, 2008
_ Rise of the Golden Dawn solo exhibition, Random Gallery, Paris, 2008
_ Curfew solo exhibition, France Fiction Galerie, Paris, 2007

AGENT
Talkie Walkie
Paris, France
www.talkiewalkie.tw

Lapin

1981 born in Chatenay-Malabry, France | lives and works in Barcelona, Spain, and Paris, France
www.lesillustrationsdelapin.com

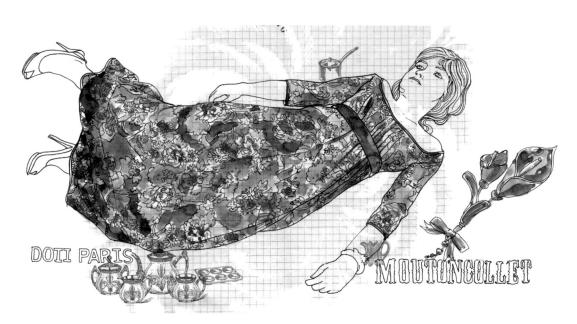

↑ *Home Alone*, catalogue, 2008, l'appart pr
→ *Very Latest Style*, 2008, personal work
→→ *Vacement Olé Olé*, promotional new year postcard, 2008, Valérie Oualid

*"With a fluid and vibrating line,
I draw my life: a collection of faces,
objects, sensations. My style is somewhere
between antique and modernity."*

*„Mit fließenden und schwingenden Linien zeichne ich mein Leben:
eine Sammlung von Gesichtern, Objekten und Empfindungen.
Mein Stil liegt irgendwo zwischen antik und modern."*

*« D'un trait fluide et vibrant, je dessine ma vie : une collection
de visages, d'objets, de sensations. Mon style se situe
quelque part entre l'ancien et le moderne. »*

TOOLS
Pen, ink, watercolour,
Adobe Photoshop

CLIENTS
Heineken, Vueling, L'appart pr,
Intermarché, Whiskas,
Paris Match, Loptimum,
Stratégies, CB News

SELECTED EXHIBITIONS
_BAC! 08 (International
Festival of Contemporary Art),
Barcelona, 2008
_Biennale du Carnet de
Voyage 08, Clermont-Ferrand,
France, 2008
_Illustrative, Paris, 2007

AGENT
Valérie Oualid
Paris, France
www.valerieoualid.com

Pablo Lobato

1970 born in Trelew, Argentina | lives and works in Buenos Aires, Argentina
www.lobaton.com.ar

"I want my portraits to be simple and efficient, something like: You know him, the guy with the long face and the crazy little eyes!"

„Ich will, dass meine Porträts einfach und effizient sind, etwa in der Art: ‚Den kennst du doch – das ist der Typ mit dem langen Gesicht und den irren kleinen Augen!'"

« Je veux que mes portraits soient simples et efficaces, quelque chose du genre ‹ Tu le connais, … tu sais, ce type à la figure allongée avec des petits yeux de dingue ! › »

↑ *Madonna*, promotional card, 2007, personal work
→ *Jack Nicholson*, 2006, Inside Entertainment Weekly
→→ *Woody Allen*, 2008, Paste magazine

TOOLS
Pencil, paper, scanner, Adobe Illustrator, Adobe Photoshop

CLIENTS
The New Yorker, Rolling Stone, Paste, Time, Texas Monthly, Chicago Tribune, New York Daily News, Cosmopolitan Munich, LA magazine, Boston Globe

SELECTED AWARDS
_ Communication Arts Illustration Annual 48/49
_ American Illustration 26/27
_ Applied Arts 2005, 2006, 2008

AGENT
Anna Goodson Management Montreal, Canada www.agoodson.com

Edna Lopes

1962 born in Curitiba, Brazil | lives and works in São Paulo and Rio de Janeiro, Brazil, and New York (NY), USA
www.ednalopes.com

↑   *Marcelo Madureira, Pinguepongue*, 2006, Vogue RG Brazil
→   *Guia RG Rio*, 2004, Vogue RG Brazil
→→ *Foresta Petrificada*, 2007, Op magazine, Portugal

*"The 'Ligne Claire' is the most obvious
influence on my work, and the first one.
Russian posters are the 'other side of the moon'..."*

*„Die ‚Ligne Claire' hat meine Arbeit am offensichtlichsten und auch am
frühesten beeinflusst. Russische Plakate sind die ‚andere Seite des Mondes' ..."*

*« La ‹ Ligne Claire › est l'influence la plus évidente de mon travail,
et la première. Les affiches russes sont ‹ la face cachée de la lune ›... »*

TOOLS
Pencil, ink, pen,
Adobe Photoshop

CLIENTS
Vogue, Op magazine

SELECTED EXHIBITIONS
_Amana Ao Deus Dará,
Cineclube Unibanco
_Amana Ao Deus Dará,
Livraria Argumento
_Entre e Ouça, 2ª Bienal dos
Quadrinhos do Brasil

Ross MacDonald

1957 born in Seaforth, Ontario, Canada | lives and works in New York (NY), USA, and Newtown (CT), USA
www.ross-macdonald.com

← *Tools of Ignorance*, "Hey Batta Batta SWING!" children's book, 2007, Simon & Schuster Publishing,
→ *Your Penis Is Shrinking!* 2000, Troika magazine
↓ *Hands Shake*, 1999, The New York Times, Op Ed page

"I like to work in a lot of different fields and media – working on the same thing all the time gets old."

„Ich arbeite gerne in vielen unterschiedlichen Bereichen und Medien – wenn man die ganze Zeit an der gleichen Sache arbeitet, wird sie alt und langweilig."

« J'aime travailler dans toutes sortes de domaines et de médias différents – toujours travailler sur les mêmes trucs fait vieillir. »

TOOLS
Brush, ink, pencil crayon, watercolour, hand printed letterpress (type and lino-cuts)

CLIENTS
The New York Times, The Wall Street Journal, Atlantic Monthly, Vanity Fair magazine, The New Yorker, The Museum of Modern Art, Walt Disney Pictures, 20th Century Fox, Universal Pictures, Touchstone Pictures, MGM

SELECTED AWARDS
_ American Illustration
_ Publishers Weekly Best Book of the Year
_ Communication Arts magazine
_ Design Excellence, Print's Regional Design Annual
_ Society of Newspaper Design

SELECTED EXHIBITIONS
_ One Man Show, The New York Times, New York, 2004
_ Illustrating the Sea, Mystic Seaport Maritime Gallery
_ Society of Illustrators National Exhibition
_ Society of Publication Designers Spots Exhibition

Emily Mackey

1976 born in London, UK | lives and works in London, UK
www.maxemilia.com

←   *Butterfly Circle*, 2008, personal work
→   *Mike*, 2008, personal work

"Embroidery has been used as a means of communication for thousands
of years. I play with perception, juxtaposing the masculine with the feminine."

„Ausschmückungen werden schon seit Tausenden von Jahren als Mittel der Kommunikation verwendet.
Ich spiele mit der Wahrnehmung und stelle das Feminine dem Maskulinen gegenüber."

« Des milliers d'années durant, la broderie a servi de moyen de communication.
Je joue avec la perception, en juxtaposant le masculin et le féminin. »

TOOLS
Sewing-machine embroidery, reverse applique, hand stitching, pen, pencil, fabric, Adobe Photoshop, Adobe Illustrator, Wacom tablet

CLIENTS
Virgin, HSBC, Orion Books, Canongate, Faber & Faber

AGENT
Dutch Uncle
London, UK
www.dutchuncle.co.uk

Sara Antoinette Martin

1983 born in Sayville, Eastern Long Island (NY), USA | lives and works in Brooklyn (NY), USA
www.saraantoinette.com

"For me, the process of creating an image is just as important as the image itself."

„Für mich ist der Prozess, ein Bild zu erschaffen, genauso wichtig wie das Bild selbst."

« Pour moi, le processus de création d'une image est aussi important que l'image elle-même. »

↑   *Sympathy*, 2008, personal work
→   *El Chupacabra Regular Edition*, vinyl toy, 2008, Kidrobot
→→ *Lady of the Sea*, 2008, personal work

TOOLS
Alkyd, acrylic, ink, Adobe Photoshop, Adobe Illustrator

CLIENTS
Kidrobot, Mishka NYC, Bust magazine, Topps

SELECTED AWARDS
_Society of Illustrators, Annual Student Scholarship Exhibition, 2005

SELECTED EXHIBITIONS
_Panorama Project 3 group show, Jonathan LeVine Gallery, New York, 2008
_Movers and Shakers group show, POV Gallery, Los Angeles, 2009
_Delineations Group Show, Ad Hoc Art, New York, 2009
_Divine Lotteria exhibition, Gowanus Studio Space Gallery, New York, 2008
_A Piece Apart group show, Aiden Savoy Gallery, New York, 2006

↑ *Abortion Rights*, 2007, Bust magazine. Art Director: Laurie Henzel
↘ *The Dating Habits of El Chupacabra*, 2008, Kidrobot
→→ *The Death of Winter*, 2008, personal work

Francisco Martins

1980 born in Lisbon, Portugal | lives and works in Lisbon, Portugal
www.subversivetales.com

↑   *Visions of Water*, personal work
↗   *Need a Hand Cinderella?*, personal work
→   *Don't be Sad Cinderella!*, personal work

*"My work is deeply inspired by the ancient mythology of the elder
civilisations, and can be dark, delicate, comic, and twisted at the same time."*

„*Meine Arbeit ist zutiefst von der uralten Mythologie früherer Zivilisationen inspiriert.
Sie kann gleichzeitig düster, feinsinnig, komisch und deformiert sein.*"

« *Mon travail est profondément inspiré par la mythologie ancienne des vieilles civilisations,
et il peut être noir, délicat, comique et tordu à la fois.* »

TOOLS
Adobe Photoshop, Adobe
Illustrator, Wacom tablet,
collage, digital painting

CLIENTS
Primitive Reason, Júlio Pereira

Maxwell

1978 born in La Rocque, Jersey, UK | lives and works in St. Helier, Jersey, and London, UK
www.maxwellillustrations.com

"Clean lines, flat colours, little or no shadow, and a slightly left-of-centre sense of humour – that just about sums it up!"

„Klare Linien, kontrastarme Farben, wenig oder kein Schatten und mit dem Humor ein wenig aus der Spur – damit ist eigentlich alles gesagt!"

« Des lignes propres, des couleurs plates, peu ou pas d'ombres et un sens de l'humour légèrement décalé – ça résume assez bien la chose ! »

↑ *Commercialisation of Religion*, 2006, Gallery magazine UK
→ *Self Delusion Has Its Uses!*, 2006, Gallery magazine UK
→→ *Amy Winehouse – Squandering Talent?*, 2007, Gallery magazine UK

TOOLS
Pencil, pen, paper, Adobe Photoshop, Wacom tablet

CLIENTS
L'Oreal, Jersey Evening Post, Liveline London, OTL Advertising, Broadlands Estates, Gallery magazine

David McLimans

1948 born in Beaver Dam (WI), USA | lives and works in Madison (WI), USA
www.davidmclimans.com

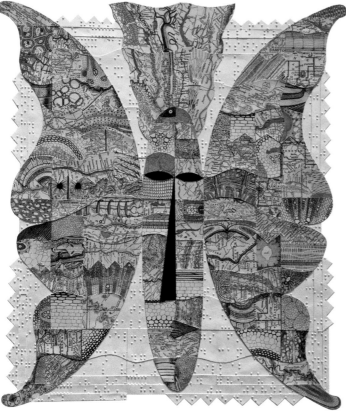

"Concepts are the impetus for my book and editorial illustrations. Design and drawing are used to clarify the underlying structure."

„Konzepte sind der Antrieb für meine redaktionellen Arbeiten und Buchillustrationen. Design und Zeichnungen sollen die zugrunde liegende Struktur verdeutlichen."

« L'élan de mes illustrations de presse et d'édition, ce sont les concepts qui le donnent. Le design et le dessin sont utilisés pour clarifier la structure sous-jacente. »

↑ *Blind Moth*, 2007, personal work
→ *Leaf Bird*, 2009, personal work
→→ *Frog Face*, 2007, personal work

TOOLS
Pencil, pen, ink, rag board, collage, watercolour, Adobe Photoshop

CLIENTS
New York Times, Harper's, Rethinking Schools, Washington Post, Walker & Company (Bloomsbury Publishing)

SELECTED AWARDS
_ Caldecott Honor
_ New York Times Best Picture Book
_ Society of Newspaper Designers Award of Excellence
_ Society of Publication Designers Award
_ Print magazine Award

SELECTED EXHIBITIONS
_ Original Art Show, Society of Illustrators
_ Best 50 books, Best 50 Covers, AIGA, New York
_ Gone Wild: An Alphabet of Endangered Animals, Woodson Art Museum
_ Another Voice: Political Art of the Late 20th Century
_ Picture This: Art from Caldecott Award Books, The Art Institute of Chicago, 2006-2009

AGENT
Melanie Jackson Agency New York, USA

Gildo Medina

1980 born in Mexico City, Mexico | lives and works in Paris, France, Brussels, Belgium, and New York (NY), USA
www.gildomedina.com

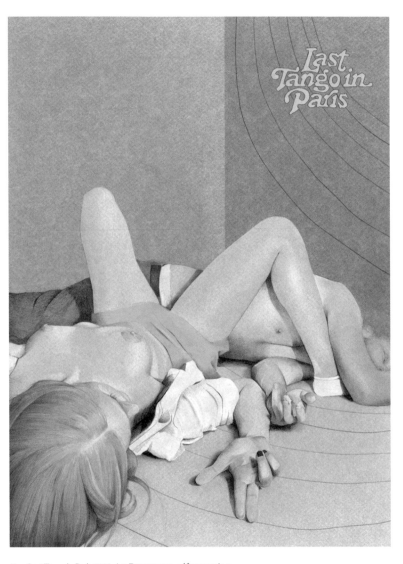

"I love to play with making photos and films, but when I draw, it is the only way to connect directly my brain, my eyes, my heart, and my hand through my pencil."

„Ich mache Fotos und Filme gerne auf spielerische Weise, aber wenn ich zeichne, ist mein Stift der einzige Weg, um eine direkte Verbindung zu meinem Gehirn, meinen Augen, meinem Herz und meiner Hand aufzubauen."

« J'aime jouer à faire des photos et des films, mais dessiner est pour moi le seul moyen de connecter directement mon cerveau, mes yeux, mon cœur et ma main au travers du crayon. »

↑ *Last Tango in Paris*, 2008, Art Department, self-promotion
↗ *Beauty Knows No Pain*, 2007, Hekmag magazine. Art Director: Thorsten Weiss
→ *Qu'est ce que je suis moche ce matin*, 2007, Hekmag magazine. Art Director: Thorsten Weiss

TOOLS
Hand drawing, graphite, marker pen, watercolour, paper, cut paper

CLIENTS
BETC EuroRCG Paris, Publicis Group, Louis Vuitton, L'Oreal Paris, Maison Fabre, Mood Media, Coca-Cola France, Fundación Medina Sidonia, Universal Music Germany, Elle magazine

SELECTED AWARDS
_ EFFIE 2007
_ MTV Video Music Awards Latin America 2004
_ The New York Festivals 2002
_ XII Entrega de Premios Quórum 2001
_ VI Entrega de Premios a! Diseño Internacional 2001

SELECTED EXHIBITIONS
_ Eat My Handbag, Puta, Gallery Chappe, Paris, 2007
_ Embassy "it" Girl, Belgian Embassy in Paris, 2007
_ Tag the System (Paris Station Espace Beaurepaire), Paris, 2005

_ Destino Común (Common Destiny), Academia de San Carlos, UNAM (Colegio Nacional de Arquitectos), 1997

AGENT
Art Department New York, USA
www.art-dept.com

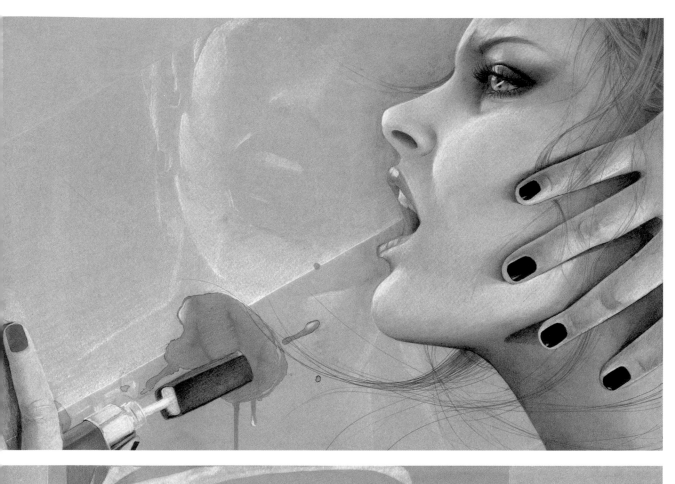

↑ *In nomine patris et filii et spiritus sancti*,
  poster, 2007, Serie A Store
→ *God save the Queen*, poster, 2007,
  Serie A Store

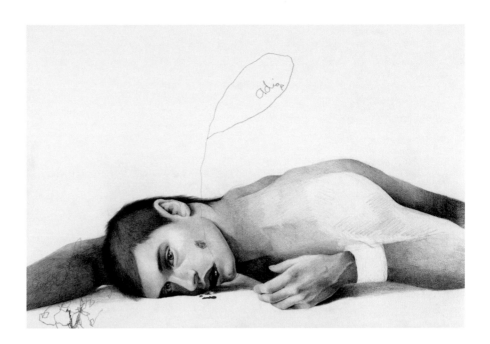

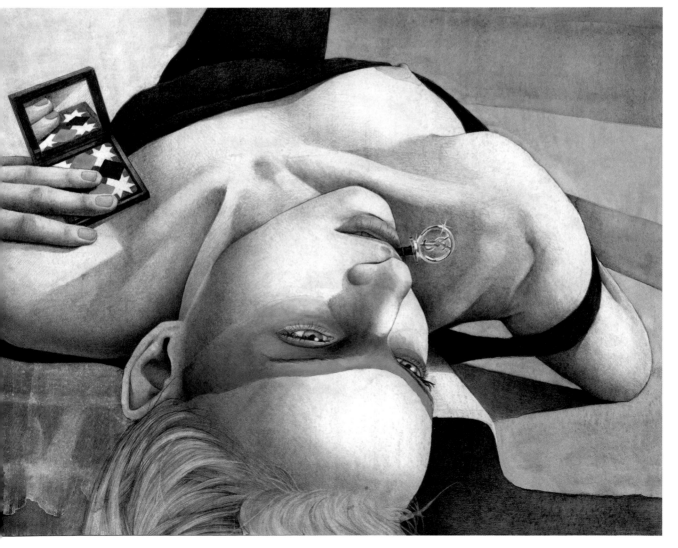

Flavio Melchiorre

1977 born in Pescara, Italy | lives and works in Città Sant'Angelo, Italy
www.flaviomelchiorre.com

↑ *Free Expression*, 2007, personal work
→ *Wild Melody*, 2008, personal work
→→ *Random World*, 2008, art-shirt, spring/summer 2008

"Free-hand drawings with chromatic and iconographic effects, producing unique results. From a single drawing many different digital elaborations may be derived. Endless, potential evolutions."

„Freihandzeichnungen mit chromatischen und ikonografischen Effekten produzieren unvergleichliche Ergebnisse. Aus einer einzigen Zeichnung können digital viele unterschiedliche Ableitungen ergearbeitet werden. Potenziell endlose Evolutionen werden möglich."

« Des dessins à main levée avec des effets chromatiques et iconographiques, qui produisent des résultats uniques. A partir d'un seul dessin, il est possible d'élaborer plusieurs différentes créations numériques. Evolutions potentielles, illimitées. »

TOOLS
Adobe Photoshop, Adobe Illustrator, Wacom tablet, digital camera

CLIENTS
Art-shirt

SELECTED AWARDS
_ OILILY Creative Studio Challenge 2008

SELECTED EXHIBITIONS
_ Segni Particolari, Pescara, Italy, 2007
_ Lineamente (Collective Exhibition), Pescara, Italy, 2005

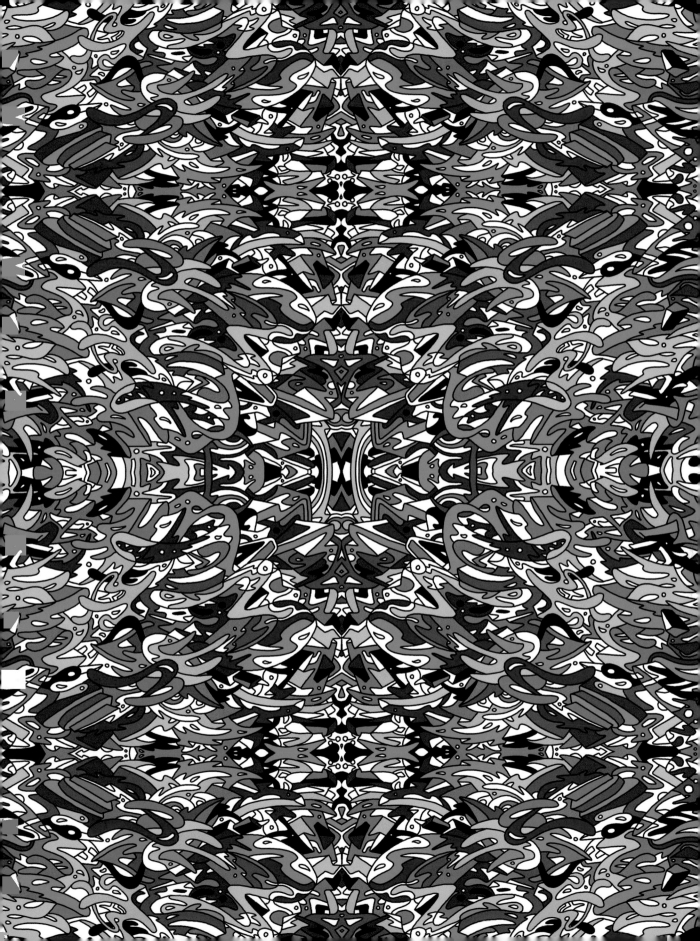

Kenzo Minami

1974 born in Hyogo, Japan | lives and works in New York (NY), USA
www.kenzominami.com

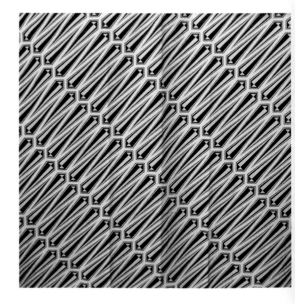

"*Schizophrenia with
precisely organized
structure and self-contained
tailor-made logic.*"

„*Eine Schizophrenie mit präzise
organisierter Struktur und
in sich geschlossener,
maßgeschneiderter Logik.*"

« *La schizophrénie, à l'intérieur d'une
structure précisément organisée,
avec une logique sur mesure indépendante.* »

↑ *Eye Dealer*, T-shirt, 2008, Garment Line Kenzo Minami
→ *MK93 (BANDANA NO.1) / Yellow*, 2008, Garment Line Kenzo Minami, Bandana Design
→→ *CLUSTER*, 2008, personal work

TOOLS
Adobe Illustrator, Adobe
Photoshop, Adobe After
Effects, print, pencil

CLIENTS
Mercedes-Benz, Microsoft,
Raf Simons, Fuse, VH1, Sharp,
Nike, Adidas, Reebok,
Converse, Hankyu, Kose,
Kidrobot, Tribeca Grand Hotel,
V magazine

SELECTED AWARDS
_ Johnnie Walker Blue Label
Celebrates 35 Under 35 2007
_ Luminaries by Lower
Manhattan Cultural Council
2006

SELECTED EXHIBITIONS
_ Famous Cars + Famous
People, 2007
_ Visionaire Gallery, 2004
_ Scope Art Fair, 2004
_ Codex 480, 2004
_ Nike Art Project Space, 2003

AGENT
CWC International
New York, USA
www.cwc-i.com

CWC
Tokyo, Japan
www.cwctokyo.com

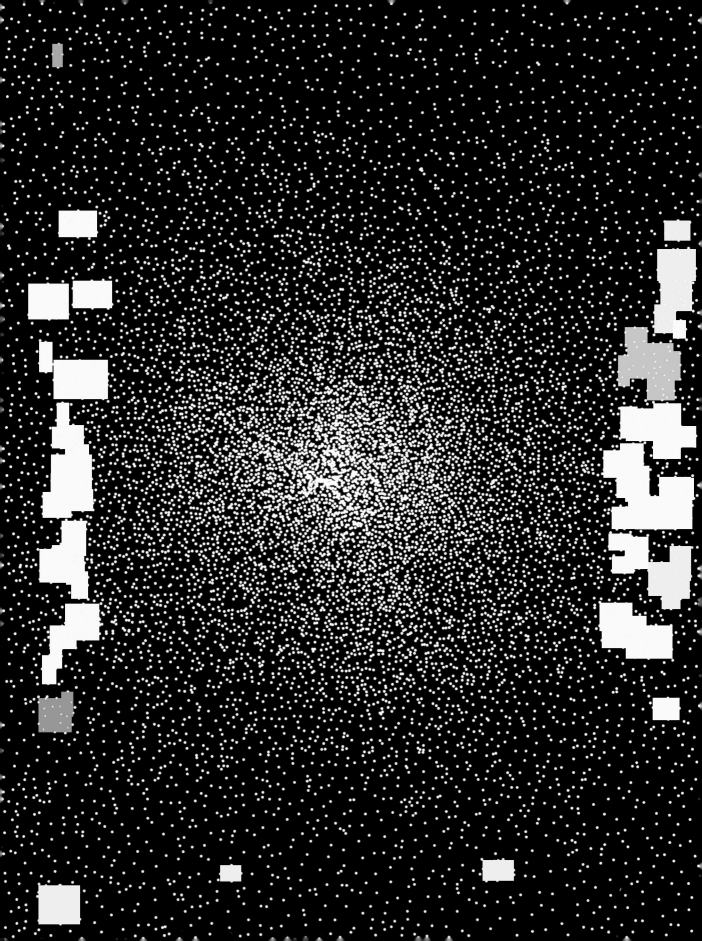

Kari Modén

1961 born in Stockholm, Sweden | lives and works in Stockholm, Sweden
www.karimoden.se

← *Infertility*, 2008, The Guardian
  Weekend magazine
  Art Director: Pauline Doyle
→ *Hair*, 2008, personal work
↓ *Love*, deck of playing cards, 2008,
  Lascivious

*"I work in a graphical way using bold
shapes and striking colours to create
my illustrations. I want my work
to be perceived as modern yet classic."*

*„Ich arbeite sehr grafisch und setze großflächige Formen
und leuchtende Farben ein, wenn ich meine Illustrationen schaffe.
Ich will, dass meine Arbeit als modern und doch klassisch betrachtet wird."*

*« J'utilise le graphisme, avec des formes brutes en gras
et des couleurs vives, pour créer mes illustrations. Je désire que mon
travail soit perçu à la fois comme moderne et classique. »*

TOOLS
Adobe Illustrator,
Wacom tablet

CLIENTS
The Guardian Weekend
magazine, Congstar, GAP,
Lascivious, Fenchurch, You
magazine, Stella magazine,
Dogs, Die Zeit, Neon
magazine, J&B Whisky,
H&M, Ikea, L'Óffcel Voyage,
Vero Moda magazine

SELECTED AWARDS
_ Kolla Award 2007
_ Svenska Tecknare Award 1995

AGENT
Peppercookies
London, UK
www.peppercookies.com

Art Liaison
Tokyo, Japan
www.art-liaison.com

Vol
Stockholm, Sweden
www.vol.se

My Dead Pony

1972 born in Charleroi, Belgium | lives and works in Brussels, Belgium | is Raphaël Vicenzi
www.mydeadpony.com

"I view my works as a blend of fashion models, symbolism, street art, melancholia, typography, and social critique."

„Ich betrachte meine Arbeiten als Mischung aus Fashionmodellen, Symbolismus, Street Art, Melancholie, Typographie und Sozialkritik."

« Je considère ce que je fais comme un mélange de modèles de mode, de symbolisme, d'art de rue, de mélancolie, de typographie et de critique sociale. »

↑   *Slave no more*, 2009, personal work
→   *I am not worthy of my shoes*, 2007, personal work
→→ *Fashion is dead*, 2008, personal work

TOOLS
Adobe Photoshop, Adobe Illustrator, Wacom tablet, blue Bic pen, watercolour, markers

CLIENTS
Undiz, String Republic, Let's Motiv, Graniph, Ride Snowboards

SELECTED EXHIBITIONS
_ Le Temp des Boutiques, Fondation Pour L'Architecture, Brussels, 2009

AGENT
Colagene
Paris, France
www.colagene.com

↗ *Morbid Fashion*, 2008, personal work
→ *Oh the slavery*, 2008, personal work
← *Flesh casket*, 2008, personal work

Fumi Nakamura

1984 born in Shizuoka, Japan | lives and works in San Francisco (CA), and New York (NY), USA
www.miniminiaturemouse.com

← *Him/Her*, book illustration, 2006, D&G, 10th Anniversary Book
→ *Struggle Against Reality and Unreality*, 2007, personal work
↓ *Let Everthing Go*, 2007, personal work

"I like to illustrate different stories and events in life with graphite pencils. The way I draw them is like creating collages, putting different objects together and building them up into one piece."

„Mit meinen Grafitstiften illustriere ich gerne verschiedene Geschichten und Geschehnisse des Lebens. Beim Zeichnen schaffe ich sozusagen Collagen, indem ich verschiedene Objekte zusammenstelle und sie in eine Gesamtheit bringe. "

« J'aime illustrer au crayon à mine de plomb différentes histoires et événements de la vie. Je m'y prends un peu comme on fait un collage, en assemblant divers éléments pour en faire une seule pièce. »

TOOLS
Graphite, coloured pencils, paper, Adobe Photoshop, lithography prints

CLIENTS
Nylon magazine, Urban Outfitters, Threadless, Graniph, GrnApple Tree Clothing, Little Pink, Bloomsbury USA/Walker Books, D&G, Nichi Bei Times

SELECTED EXHIBITIONS
_ Solo Exhibition, The National Grid Gallery, Sydney, 2009
_ Himitsu solo exhibition, DDR Project, Long Beach, California, 2007
_ Curvy Three, DAS Gallery, Sydney, 2006

_ For You, Servicio Ejecutivo, New York, 2006
_ Sketchel, Semi-Permanents, Sydney, 2005

Barbara Nessim

1939 born in New York (NY), USA | lives and works in New York (NY), USA
www.barbaranessim.com

← *Personal Number*, residential building lobby, 2006, Perkins Eastman Architects, commissioned by Philip Koether
→ *Curious Secret*, residential building lobby, 2004, Costas Kondylis Architects, commissioned by Philip Koether

"Releasing my creative potential is about relaxing my conscious thought process, paying attention to my peripheral vision, and taking action."

„Wenn ich mein kreatives Potenzial freisetze, geht es darum, das bewusste Denken zu entspannen, auf die periphere Sichtweise zu achten und dann ins Handeln zu kommen."

« Pour moi, lâcher la bride au potentiel de création consiste à détendre le processus de pensée consciente, faire attention à la vision périphérique et agir. »

TOOLS
Pen, ink, watercolour, gouache, pastels, Adobe Creative Suite, digital painting on canvas, oil, acrylic, etching, collage

CLIENTS
Time magazine, Rolling Stone, The New York Times, Frankfurter Allgemeine Zeitung, Ralph Lauren, Levi's, Doubleday, New York magazine, Newsweek, Boston Globe, Chicago Tribune, Glamour, Travel + Leisure, Self

SELECTED AWARDS
_ Communication Arts Illustration Annual 46
_ Society of Publication Designers 1998
_ American Illustration 6th Competition 1986
_ ACM Siggraph Grant 1990
_ International Digitart Competition, Hungary 1990

SELECTED EXHIBITIONS
_ Transition, Sienna Gallery, Lenox, MA, 2007
_ Black Truths/White Lies, curated by Steven Sacks, Bitforms Gallery, NY, 2003
_ Random Access Memories, USA/Colombia, 1991–1994
_ Artware/Kunst Electronic, curated by David Galloway, Hanover, 1989
_ The Work of Barbara Nessim, Shiseido Ginza Gallery, Tokyo, 1986

Franziska Neubert

1977 born in Leipzig, Germany | lives and works in Leipzig, Germany
www.franziska-neubert.de

← *Puppet*, book, 2007,
  Éditions Thierry Magnier
  Art Director: Valerie Cusaguet
→ *Greta*, 2007, personal work
↓ *Lucie à Paris II*, 2008, book

"The respect shown by the future viewer should not lead to a situation in which all expectations are fulfilled, but rather create something new, perhaps even unexpected."

„Der dem zukünftigen Betrachter gezollte Respekt sollte nicht zu einer Situation führen, in der alle Erwartungen erfüllt werden, sondern vielmehr etwas Neues, vielleicht gar Unerwartetes geschaffen wird."

« Le respect envers le futur spectateur ne devrait pas conduire à une situation dans laquelle toutes les attentes sont comblées, mais plutôt créer quelque chose de nouveau, voire peut-être d'inattendu. »

TOOLS
Papercuts, woodcuts, serigraphy, mixed media

CLIENTS
Éditions Thierry Magnier, Wagenbach-Verlag Berlin, Éditions La Maison est en Carton

SELECTED AWARDS
_ Best Designed Books in Germany 2007
_ Ars Lipsiensis 2007
_ Walter-Tiemann-Prize 2008

SELECTED EXHIBITIONS
_ Building and Urban Affairs, Federal Ministry of Transport, Berlin, 2008
_ Galerie 18m, Berlin, 2008
_ Selected Bologna Illustrators, Chicago, 2009

_ Bologna Illustrators Exhibition, Italy/Japan/Korea, 2007/2008
_ Futur Figur, Paris, 2006

AGENT
Bridgeman Art Library Berlin, Germany
www.bridgemanart.de

Pawel Nolbert

1984 born in Wieruszow, Poland | lives and works in Warsaw, Poland
www.hellocolor.com

"My style is very much diversified by the wide spectrum of my inspirations and interests. That diversification is reflected in a rich use of colours and forms"

„Mein Stil ist durch das große Spektrum meiner Interessen und Inspirationen sehr breit gefächert. Dem entspricht der vielseitige Einsatz von Formen und Farben."

« L'ampleur du spectre de mes inspirations et de mes intérêts explique l'extrême diversité de mon style. Cette diversité, l'usage généreux que je fais des couleurs et des formes, la reflète. »

↑ *Naturally Create*, 2008, personal work
→ *Chocolatopia*, 2008, personal work
→→ *Untitled*, cover, 2007, Kudos magazine

TOOLS
Adobe Photoshop,
Wacom tablet, pencil,
Discreet 3ds Max,
Adobe Flash

CLIENTS
Citroen, Nike, Motorola,
Esquire, Bacardi, Coca-Cola,
Deutsche Post, McDonald's,
Unilever, Nutricia, Glaceau,
Future Publishing, DDB,
Metaphrenie, EPOS, Vizualogic

SELECTED AWARDS
_ Favourite Website Awards
_ Dope Award
_ Design TAXI Site of the Day

Oh Yeah Studio

2008 founded in Oslo, Norway | is Christina Magnussen & Hans Christian Oren
www.ohyeahstudio.no

"*The essentials in our design are abstract and geometric shapes fused with the hand-drawn. We also have a palette of few colours.*"

„Bei unserem Design verwenden wir hauptsächlich abstrakte und geometrische Formen, die mit Handzeichnungen verschmelzen. Wir arbeiten außerdem mit einer kleinen Farbpalette."

« Les essentiels de notre design sont les formes géométriques fondues avec du dessin manuel. Nous avons aussi une palette de quelques couleurs. »

↑   *Abstract*, T-shirt illustration, 2008, Ministry of Press
→   *Be more creative*, 2008, Computer Arts UK/Finland
→→ *Tiger*, T-shirt illustration, 2008, Ministry of Press

TOOLS
Pencil, paper, Adobe Photoshop, Adobe Illustrator, scanner, digital camera, Wacom tablet

CLIENTS
Computer Arts, D2, Ministry of Press, Sony Ericsson, Burton, London Innovation Centre, Kunstmuseene i Bergen, Monster

SELECTED AWARDS
_ Interactive Design 2008 Visuelt, nomination
_ Illustration Gullblyantspisseren 2005–2006
_ Open Text Gullblyantspisseren 2005

SELECTED EXHIBITIONS
_ Whaleless, Italy, 2008
_ Three Weeks, Oslo, 2008
_ Dashed Lines, Bergen, 2007
_ New Talents Doga, Oslo, 2007
_ Bikeshed, London, 2006

↑   *Whaleless*, 2008, Giovanni Cervi,
    The Whaleless Project
→   *I am man*, 2008, D2 magazine
←   *Eye*, T-shirt illustration, 2008,
    Ministry of Press

Patricio Oliver

1977 born in Zapala, Argentina | lives and works in Buenos Aires, Argentina
www.patriciooliver.com.ar

"I'm not an illustrator. I'm just a medium between my obscure characters and the real world. I'm just the tool that helps them manifest themselves."

„Ich bin kein Illustrator, sondern nur das Medium zwischen meinen obskuren Figuren und der realen Welt. Ich bin bloß das Instrument, das den Figuren hilft, sich zu manifestieren."

« Je ne suis pas un illustrateur. Juste un intermédiaire entre mes personnages obscurs et le monde réel. Juste un instrument qui les aide à se manifester par eux-mêmes. »

↑ *DO uble star E*, 2008, personal work
→ *Priotcia*, magazine cover, 2008, Impulso Cultural magazine
→→ *Ro jo en SHOCK*, 2008, personal work

TOOLS
Adobe Illustrator, Wacom tablet

CLIENTS
Red Magic, Kidrobot, Rolling Stone magazine Argentina, Brando magazine, Mutek Festival, Moebius Editora, Upper Case Gallery, Pink Ghost Gallery, Ediciones Quipu

SELECTED EXHIBITIONS
_The Robot Show, Uppercase Gallery, Calgary, Canada
_Buenos Aires Urban Art Festival
_Villains & More Villains Show, PinkGhost, Fort Lauderdale, Florida, USA
_The Little Bird Project, j3fm Gallery, Hannover, Germany
_mixtART, Giant Robot, San Francisco

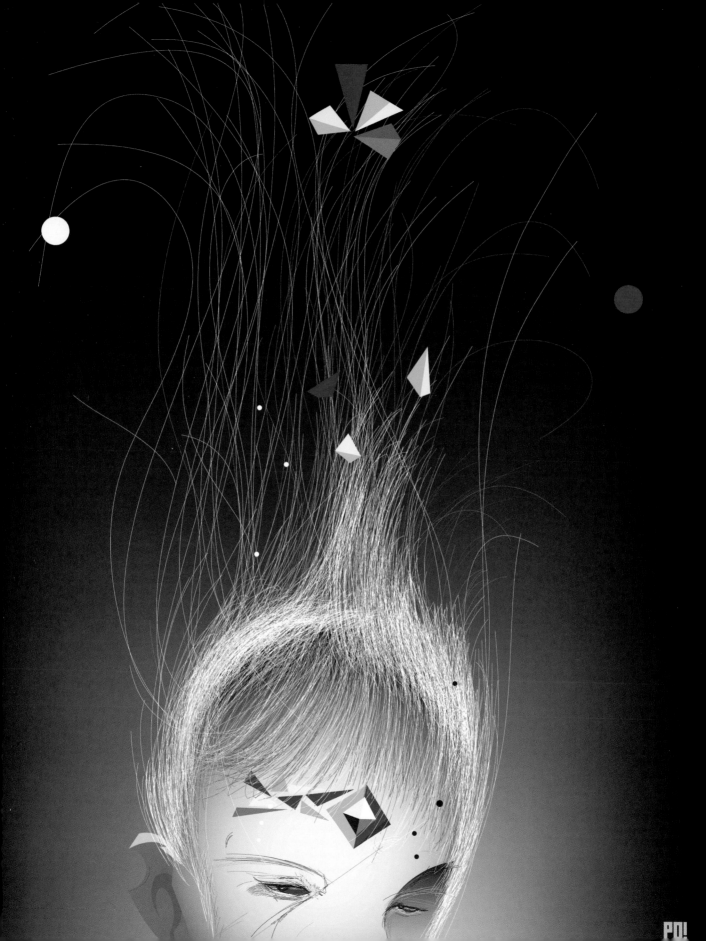

Onesidezero

2005 born in Worcestershire, UK | lives and works in Leicester, UK | is Brett Wilkinson
www.onesidezero.co.uk

← *Vortex*, 2009, DJ Slipmat
→ *Surrounded by Colours*, postcard, 2008, personal work
↓ *Tuba Monster*, 2008, personal work

*"My imagination is a realm of shapes,
colours, and curious personalities.
I illustrate to capture a state of mind,
full of happiness and memories."*

*„Meine Vorstellungskraft steckt voller Formen,
Farben und merkwürdigen Persönlichkeiten.
Ich illustriere, um einen Bewusstseinszustand einzufangen
– voller Glück und Zufriedenheit und Erinnerungen."*

*« Mon imagination est un royaume de formes,
de couleurs et d'étranges personnalités. J'illustre pour
capturer un état d'esprit, plein de bonheur et de souvenirs. »*

TOOLS
Adobe Photoshop, Adobe
Illustrator, pen, pencil

CLIENTS
4Talent, Amelia's magazine,
Big Chill Festival, Wallcandy

SELECTED EXHIBITIONS
_ Facelift, London/Hong Kong,
2008
_ Inkthis 2, London, 2007
_ Semi-Permanent, Sydney,
2007

AGENT
Advocate
London, UK
www.advocate-art.com

Mia Marie Overgaard

1978 born in Copenhagen, Denmark | lives and works in Copenhagen, Denmark, and Rochester (NY), USA
www.miaovergaard.com

↑   *Alice*, website, 2008, Prestigium Group
    Art Director: Lavinia Schimmelpenninck
→   *Red*, 2007, personal work
→→ *Culture*, 2008, personal work

*"I have a very serious relationship
with my pencil. We have been living
and working together for years
and I am still very much in love!"*

*„Ich führe eine sehr enge und intensive Beziehung mit
meinem Bleistift. Wir leben und arbeiten bereits seit
Jahren zusammen, und ich bin immer noch sehr verliebt!"*

*« J'entretiens une relation très sérieuse avec mon crayon.
Nous vivons et travaillons ensemble depuis des années,
et j'en suis toujours très amoureuse ! »*

TOOLS
Pencil, ink, watercolour,
acrylic, airbrush, Adobe
Photoshop

CLIENTS
Air Canada/EnRoute, Amelia's
magazine, Anova Books,
CosmoGIRL!, Fused magazine,
Mao Mao Publishing, Marie
Claire, Neiman Marcus, RSCG
Ad Agency, SELF magazine,
The Perfect Kiss Records

SELECTED EXHIBITIONS
_ Orange Dot Gallery & Favela
Chic (collective exhibition),
London, 2007
_ FrenchTrotters solo
exhibition, Paris, 2007
_ Pure Groove (collective
exhibition), London, 2008

AGENT
Peppercookies
London, UK
www.peppercookies.com

Traffic Creative Management
New York, USA
www.trafficnyc.com

Creative Syndicate
Paris, France
www.creative-syndicate.com

Pietari Posti

1979 born in Helsinki, Finland | lives and works in Barcelona, Spain
www.pposti.com

"Drawing for me is like meditating. When I'm drawing, I forget the rest of the world, and enter a new one."

„Zeichnen ist für mich wie Meditieren. Wenn ich zeichne, vergesse ich die restliche Welt und betrete eine neue."

« Pour moi, dessiner s'apparente à la méditation. J'oublie le reste du monde quand je dessine, pour pénétrer dans un autre. »

↑ *When the man doesn't feel like it*, 2008, Olivia magazine
Art Director: Tuomas Jääskeläinen
→ *Metropolis*, poster, 2008, Type by Underware
→→ *Circus*, book illustration, 2008, American Express/VSA Partners
Art Director: Jennifer Lee

TOOLS
Mixed media, Indian ink, pencil, Adobe Photoshop, Wacom tablet

CLIENTS
American Airlines, Playboy, The New York Times, New York magazine, National Geographic, The Washington Post, The Los Angeles Times, The Guardian, Business Week, Urban Outfitters, Dazed & Confused

SELECTED AWARDS
_ American Illustration 27
_ 3x3 magazine
_ PRINT magazine European Annual 2007

SELECTED EXHIBITIONS
_ Giants! solo exhibition, Dudua, Barcelona, 2008
_ Kokeshi: From Folk Art to Art Toy, The Japanese American National Museum, Los Angeles, 2009
_ Cut It Out Exhibition, Open Space Gallery, New York, 2009

AGENT
Agent002
Paris, France
www.agent002.com

Debut Art
London, UK
www.debutart.com

2Agenten
Berlin, Germany
www.2agenten.com

↑ *Fashion in Art*, 2008, j'n'c magazine
→ *GIANTS!*, magazine cover, 2007, Helsinki Design Week

Unglued, 2008, Paste magazine

Ulla Puggaard

1968 born in Copenhagen, Denmark | lives and works in London, UK

Bodyworks, 2007, exhibition Designers Block London

→ *Radio town*, 2008, The Guardian

→→ *The face*, T-shirt, 2006, Topshop

"Graphic and bold, voyeuristic and suggestive, where the empty space plays a big part in the relationship between space, forms, and colours."

„Grafisch und gewagt, voyeuristisch und suggestiv – der leere Raum spielt eine wichtige Rolle in der Beziehung zwischen Raum, Formen und Farben."

« Graphique et gras, voyeuriste et suggestif, où les espaces vides jouent un grand rôle dans la relation entre l'espace, les formes et couleurs. »

TOOLS

Ink, paint, pencil, paper, canvas, print and lino-cuts mixed with hand rendering, Wacom tablet

CLIENTS

The New Yorker, The New York Times, The Telegraph, The Observer, The Guardian, UPS, ESPN, Marie Claire, Elle Decoration, Habitat, Wallpaper, Topshop, Comme des Garçons, Coca-Cola, VW, Peugeot, Hyundai, Vodafone

SELECTED AWARDS

_American Illustration
_Images UK 2008
_Communication Arts magazine
_Applied Arts 2005
_D&AD 2002

SELECTED EXHIBITIONS

_Designers Block, UK, 2007
_S-magazine Launch Show, USA, 2006
_The Hoxton Show, UK, 2008
_CIA Summershow, UK, 2008
_Apart Gallery, UK, 2003

AGENT

Kate Larkworthy Artist Representation
New York, USA
www.larkworthy.com

Tomorrow Management
Copenhagen, Denmark
tomorrowmanagement.com

Central Illustration
London, UK
www.centralillustration.com

↑   *Not war*, 2008, S-magazine, Copenhagen
←   *Man on Chair*, 2005, The Guardian

Crystal Meth, campaign for Vodafone, 2007,
The New York Times
Kafka, 2008, The Telegraph

Cédric Quissola

1982 born in Marseille, France | lives and works in Paris, France
http://cedric.quissola.site.voila.fr

"If I had to label my work, I would combine terms which otherwise do not agree with another: figurative abstraction."

„Wenn ich meine Arbeit beschreiben müsste, würde ich Begriffe miteinander kombinieren, die sich ansonsten nicht vertragen würden: figürliche Abstraktion."

« Si je devais étiqueter mon travail, j'associerais des termes par ailleurs contradictoires : abstraction figurative. »

↑   *Not so Lucky*, 2008, personal work
→   *Motel*, 2008, personal work
→→ *What are pastas really made with?*, 2008, personal work

TOOLS
Coloured pencils

CLIENTS
Etapes magazine, Milk magazine, Jalouse magazine, Le Monde

SELECTED AWARDS
_ Young Illustrators Award
_ École Spéciale d'Architecture 2008

SELECTED EXHIBITIONS
_ Illustrative Paris, 2007
_ Passion D'images Festival, Marseille, 2008
_ Biennale Internationale Design, Saint-Étienne, 2008
_ Illustrative Zurich, 2008
_ Play List, Galerie Patricia Dorfmann, Paris, 2008

AGENT
Talkie Walkie
Paris, France
www.talkiewalkie.tw

What are pastas really made with?

Le complexe de l'aspiration

↑   *Le complexe de l'aspiration*, 2008, personal work
←   *L'amour et l'autorité*, 2008, Milk magazine

Natalie Ratkovski

1977 born in Stanitsa, Russia | lives and works in Hattingen, Germany
www.floaty.de

"To illustrate is a form of movement for me. If I don't draw, I have a feeling I am standing still."

„Illustrieren ist für mich eine Bewegungsform. Wenn ich nicht zeichne, habe ich das Gefühl stillzustehen."

« Pour moi, illustrer est une forme en mouvement. Si je ne dessine pas, j'ai l'impression d'être immobile. »

↑ *Excessive Shopping in Paris*, 2008, I BUY magazine, Russia
→ *Oil Business and Richness, Part #1*, 2008, CFO magazine, Russia
→→ *Homage to Gary Baseman*, 2007, personal work

TOOLS
Pen, paper, Adobe Photoshop,
Wacom tablet

CLIENTS
Cosmopolitan Beauty Russia,
CFO Russia, The Health
magazine Russia, Maxim
Russia, opta data Gruppe
Germany, PC Mobile Russia,
Russian Life magazine,
Vogue Russia

Rocco

1962 born in Metz, France | lives and works in Paris, France

"Let's see!" — Gus Bofa

„Lass uns mal schauen!"

« On verra bien ! »

↑ *The Art Director*, 2008, magazine illustration
→ *Wawa Color*, comic book cover, 2007, Sortez La Chienne Comics
→→ *Who's Afraid of…*, magazine illustration

TOOLS
Adobe Photoshop,
Adobe Illustrator

CLIENTS
Canal+, Mikros Image,
BNP Paribas, ICADE, AFOM,
Libération, Le Monde

SELECTED EXHIBITIONS
_ Sous Presse, Arts Factory
(Galerie Nomade), Paris, 2000
_ Fresh Art, Galerie
Lavignes-Bastille, Paris, 2002
_ Graphic Session, Espace EOF,
Paris, 2006

AGENT
La Superette
Paris, France
www.lasuperette.com

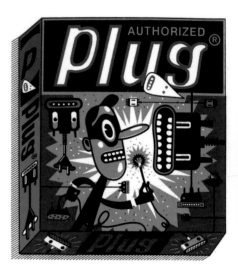

← *Smokey*, 200/, personal work
→ *Le Fantôme de l'apéro*, DVD cover, 2008,
   Mikros Image/Canal+
↓ *Plug*, 2007, personal work

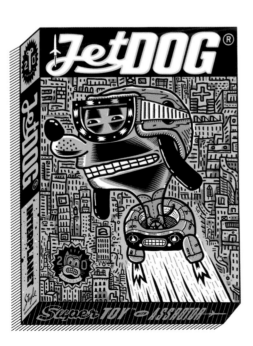

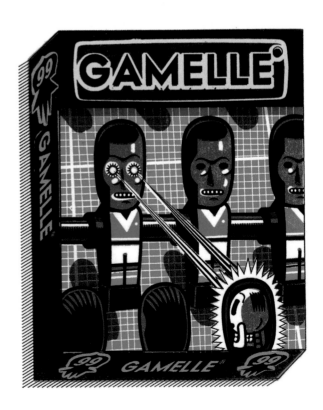

↑ *Jetdog*, 2007, personal work
→ *Gamelle*, 2007, personal work

André Rösler

1970 born in Lahr, Germany | lives and works in Karlsruhe, Germany
www.der-roesler.de

*"I draw only with my mouth.
I curse and steal ideas. I focus on
a point on the horizon and hum
a melody. Digital and analog!"*

*„Ich zeichne ausschließlich mit dem Mund. Ich fluche
und klaue Ideen. Ich fixiere einen Punkt am Horizont,
und summe eine Melodie. Digital und analog!"*

*« Je dessine uniquement avec ma bouche. Je jure
et je vole des idées. Je fixe un point à l'horizon et
je murmure une mélodie. Numérique et analogique ! »*

↑   *Hands*, 2008, personal work
→   *Untitled*, exhibition wall, detail, 2008, Illustrative Festival
→→ *Untitled*, exhibition wall, detail, 2008, Illustrative Festival

TOOLS
Pen, acrylic, paper,
Adobe Photoshop, Adobe
Illustrator, Wacom tablet

CLIENTS
Frankfurter Allgemeine
Zeitung, Bayerischer
Rundfunk, Jung von Matt/
Kempertrautmann GmbH,
Musikexpress, Limmat AG,
Slanted Magazin, Springer
& Jacoby Design GmbH

SELECTED AWARDS
_Art Directors Club
Switzerland 1998
_Art Directors Club Germany
2005
_Creative Review 2005
_One Show Award 2005

SELECTED EXHIBITIONS
_Illustrative, Zurich, 2008
_Illustrative, Berlin, 2007
_Colophon International
magazine Symposium,
Casino Luxembourg Forum
d'art Contemporain, 2007
_Pictoplasma Conference,
Berlin, 2006

_Bastard Project Show,
Ras Gallery, Barcelona, 2006

Sonia Roy

1975 born in Montreal, Quebec, Canada | lives and works in Montreal, Quebec, Canada

↑ *Bad Trip*, 2008, Globe and Mail
→ *Portrait de Charles Darwin*, 2008, Philosophie magazine

"I love working with texture, colour, and symbols. To create my collages, I use mostly archive photographs, because I find them rich and poetic."

„Ich liebe es, mit Texturen, Farben und Symbolen zu arbeiten. Für meine Collagen verwende ich hauptsächlich Archivfotos, weil ich finde, dass sie so vielfältig und poetisch sind."

« J'adore travailler avec les textures, les couleurs et les symboles. Pour mes collages, j'utilise principalement des photos d'archives, car je les trouve plus riches et poétiques. »

TOOLS
Adobe Photoshop,
digital camera

CLIENTS
Los Angeles Times, The
Washington Post, Globe and
Mail, Entertainment Weekly,
BusinessWeek, Detroit Hour
magazine, Vancouver
magazine, Out magazine,
TAXI, L'Européen

AGENT
Colagene
Montreal, Canada
Paris, France
www.colagene.com

Loïc Sattler

1980 born in Saverne, France | lives and works in Paris, France | also known as Lysergid
www.lysergid.com

"*To be understood as an individual who wishes to take things further by empowering the profession to the best of its ability.*"

„*Ich will als Individuum verstanden werden, das die Dinge vorantreiben will, indem aus der Profession das Optimum herausgeholt wird.*"

« *Etre compris comme une personne désireuse de faire avancer les choses en permettant à la profession d'exercer au mieux ses talents.* »

↑ *Untitled*, magazine cover, 2008, Goma magazine, Brazil
→ *LSD for Magu*, 2009, Magu-Design
→→ *Untitled*, book Semi-Permanent, 2008, Design is Kinky, Australia

---

TOOLS
Digital camera, scanner, tablet, paper, pencils, 3D Studio Max, Cinema 4D, Adobe Illustrator, Adobe Photoshop, After Effects, Adobe InDesign

CLIENTS
Adidas, Coca-Cola, Burn, Design Council London, BMW, IBM, SFR, SNCF, L'Oreal, Triumph, Warner Bros, Yamaha, Unicef, Procter & Gamble, LcL, Freedent, Score Game, Sony, Masterfoods, Armani, Dolce&Gabbana

SELECTED AWARDS
_ FWA
_ FITC Canada
_ Computerlove
_ Netdiver
_ Ventilate

SELECTED EXHIBITIONS
_ Apple Expo, Paris
_ Lazy Dog Paris, Paris
_ Menas Art Gallery, Switzerland
_ OFFF Exhibition, Lisbon
_ Gallery 27, London

Matthias Schardt

1972 born in Hadamar, Germany | lives and works in Düsseldorf, Germany
www.schardt-illustration.de

← *Ratzinger*, personal work
→ *The Stranger*, personal work
↓ *Ornette Coleman*, personal work

"Striving for a tension-filled and intuitive style, it is the delicacy and flexibility of the brush stroke which is the essence of my illustrations."

„Ich strebe einen spannungsreichen und intuitiven Stil an, wobei Feinheit und Flexibilität des Pinselstrichs die Essenz meiner Illustrationen bildet."

« En quête d'un style intuitif et nerveux, la délicatesse et la souplesse du pinceau sont l'essence de mes illustrations. »

TOOLS
Indian ink, brush, pencil, Adobe Photoshop

CLIENTS
Siemens, VW, Bosch, Castrol, Vodafone, Toyota, Daihatsu, Köstritzer, Orbit, Schüler Helfen Leben e.V., Germanwings

AGENT
Kombinatrotweiss Frankfurt, Germany www.kombinatrotweiss.de

Jason Seiler

1977 born in Green Bay (WI), USA | lives and works in Chicago (IL), USA
www.levycreative.com

"I truly enjoy drawing and painting people, and capturing their truth in exaggerated form. Everyone is unique, and I thrive on that."

„Ich genieße es von tiefstem Herzen, Menschen zu zeichnen und zu malen und dabei ihre Wahrheit in übertriebener Form einzufangen. Jeder ist völlig einzigartig, und ich ziehe daraus einen großen Gewinn."

« Je prends vraiment du plaisir à dessiner et peindre les gens, à saisir leur vérité en forçant le trait. Tout le monde est unique, et c'est ce que j'exploite. »

↑ *Jim Jones*, 2009, KING magazine
→ *Sundays with Tiger*, 2007, Golf magazine
→→ *Madoff*, 2009, The New York Times

TOOLS
Acrylic paint, oil paint, watercolour, digital painting

CLIENTS
MAD magazine, Time magazine, New York Times, The Weekly Standard, The Village Voice, Bloomberg, Business Week, Guitar Player, Chicago, Revolver, Minnesota Monthly, Wine & Spirits, Universal Pictures

SELECTED AWARDS
_ Gold Nosey Award, Guest of Honor Award, Caricature of the Year: International Society of Caricature Artists 17th Annual
_ CG Choice Award, Society of Digital Artists

SELECTED EXHIBITIONS
_ Society of Illustrators, 49th Annual, American Illustration Show
_ Society of Illustrators West, 46th and 47th Annual Show
_ The Caricature's World Exhibit, Alive Gallery, Seoul, South Korea

AGENT
Levy Creative Management New York, USA
www.levycreative.com

Natsko Seki

1976 born in Tokyo, Japan | lives and works in London, UK
www.natsko.com

← *Circus – Whimsical Orchestra*, 2008, personal work
→ *London*, 2007, personal work
↓ *Great Wheel*, 2007, personal work

"Love of antique and vintage culture gives my illustrations a nostalgic feel, and this combined with employing mixed-media techniques using my own photographs and drawings makes them contemporary at the same time."

„Meine Liebe zu antiken und altmodischen Kulturen verleiht meinen Illustrationen eine nostalgische Anmutung. In Kombination mit Mixed-Media-Techniken, bei denen ich eigene Fotos und Zeichnungen verwende, werden meine Illustrationen gleichzeitig auch zeitgenössisch."

« L'amour pour la culture ancienne et antique donne à mes illustrations une note nostalgique, et ceci, allié à des techniques multimédias et à mes propres photos et dessins, les rend en même temps contemporaines. »

TOOLS
Pentel automatic pencils, tracing papers, Adobe Photoshop, digital camera, Wacom tablet

CLIENTS
Louis Vuitton Japan, Yahoo! Japan, Muji UK, The Guardian, The New York Times, Wallpaper, Elle Decoration, Vogue Nippon, Bloomsbury Publishing, Fukuinkan, London Fire Brigade

SELECTED AWARDS
_ Mainichi Advertisement Design Competition

SELECTED EXHIBITIONS
_ Retro Perspective solo exhibition, Gallery Rocket, Tokyo, 2008
_ Rose Tinted Spectacles, Designersblock, London, 2007
_ 6 Impossible Things, Nolias Gallery, London, 2007

AGENT
Agency Rush
Brighton, UK
www.agencyrush.com

Taiko & Associates
Tokyo, Japan
www.ua-net.com/taiko

Agent 002
Paris, France
www.agent002.com

Koren Shadmi

1981 born in Kfar Saba, Israel | lives and works in Brooklyn (NY), USA
www.korenshadmi.com

"In my work I try to put the same emphasis on the visual landscape as I do on the conceptual elements which together comprise the whole."

„In meiner Arbeit versuche ich, der visuellen Landschaft die gleiche Betonung zu geben wie den konzeptuellen Elementen, die zusammengenommen ein Ganzes werden."

« Dans mon travail, je tâche de mettre en valeur aussi bien le paysage visuel que les éléments conceptuels qui constituent le tout. »

↑   *Untitled*, 2008, King magazine
→   *The Sock War*, promotional poster, 2008, personal work
→→ *Atlanta*, children's book illustration, 2007, Kineret Books

---

TOOLS
Pencil, ink, watercolour,
Adobe Photoshop

CLIENTS
Spin magazine, BusinessWeek,
The Village Voice, The Boston
Globe, The New York Times,
The Progressive, The San
Francisco Chronicle, ESPN,
Mother Jones

SELECTED AWARDS
_ Albert Dorne Award,
Society of Illustrators
_ Primo Gran Guinigi 2008
_ Gilbert Stone Scholarship
_ Shakespeare & Co Grant
2006

SELECTED EXHIBITIONS
_ Herzelia Biennial, Israel, 2008
_ Helsinki Biennial, 2008
_ Artists Against The War,
Society of Illustrators, 2008
_ Take the Baasa with Sababa,
Israeli Illustrators exhibition,
London, 2008

Cristiano Siqueira

1979 born in São Paulo, Brazil | lives and works in São Paulo, Brazil
www.crisvector.com

"I try to create images that say more than the obvious. I want my work to survive after its publication so that it can be appreciated for longer."

„Ich versuche Bilder zu schaffen, die mehr als das Offensichtliche sagen. Ich will, dass meine Arbeiten auch nach ihrer Veröffentlichung lebensfähig sind, damit sie länger gewürdigt werden."

« J'essaie de créer des images qui disent davantage que l'évidence. Je veux que mon travail survive après sa publication afin de pouvoir être apprécié plus longtemps. »

↑ *Ad Infinitum*, poster, 2008, personal work
→ *King*, poster, 2007, personal work
→→ *Le Chapeau Noir*, poster, 2008, personal work

TOOLS
Digital tools, Wacom tablet, Adobe Photoshop, Poser, Adobe Illustrator

CLIENTS
Editora Abril, Tetra Pak, Aché, Richmond Publishing, Del Valle, Ultra Music Festival, Calçados Azaléia

SELECTED AWARDS
_ Deviousness Award, DeviantArt.com
_ Projeto Carta Branca, Mica Postcards
_ DepthCore Digital Art Group, featured artist of the chapter Temple

SELECTED EXHIBITIONS
_ Brasilidade Ilustrada, IED (Istituto Europeo di Design)
_ 115 Digital Art Gallery

Elwood H. Smith

1941 born in Alpena (MI), USA | lives and works in Rhinebeck (NY), USA
www.elwoodsmith.com

↑ *Free Chortles*, 2006, self-promotion
→ *Animal Waste Management*, 2002, Fortune magazine
→→ *Waiting for the Other Shoe*, 2000, self-promotion

"Growing up, my heroes were Krazy Kat and Barney Google, and now, like them, I make my living drawing silly, madcap pictures."

„Als ich klein war, waren Krazy Kat und Barney Google meine Helden, und heute lebe ich davon, alberne, spinnerte Bilder wie sie zu zeichnen."

« Quand j'étais môme, mes héros étaient Krazy Kat et Barney Google, et maintenant, comme eux, je gagne ma vie en dessinant des âneries. »

TOOLS
Watercolour, India ink, watercolour paper, Adobe Photoshop, Wacom tablet, Toon Boom Studio

CLIENTS
Time magazine, Newsweek, Wall Street Journal, Simon & Schuster, Viking, NY Times, Fast Company, Fortune, Forbes, Boston Globe, Washington Post, Sierra magazine, QVC, Ameristar, Samsung, Hasbro

SELECTED AWARDS
_ Society of Illustrators
_ Print magazine
_ Communication Arts magazine
_ Art Direction magazine
_ The Art Directors Club

SELECTED EXHIBITIONS
_ Gallery Z solo exhibition, New York
_ Society of Illustrators
_ Art Directors Club
_ The Norman Rockwell Museum
_ The Illustration Gallery, New York

AGENT
Maggie Pickard
Rhinebeck, USA
www.littlewonderdesign.com

Nina Soentgerath

1981 born in Nuremberg, Germany | lives and works in Nuremberg, Germany
www.kilioa.de

"My works are affected by the glamorous Seventies, as well as by places I have travelled to, where I became acquainted with different cultures and their lifestyles."

„Meine Arbeiten sind von den glamourösen Siebzigern beeinflusst, aber auch von Orten, die ich bereist habe und an denen ich mich mit verschiedenen Kulturen und ihren Lebensstilen vertraut machen durfte."

« Ce que je fais est très influencé par le glamour des années soixante-dix, ainsi que par certains endroits que j'ai visités, où j'ai fait connaissance avec différentes cultures et leurs modes de vie. »

↑ *Eyecatcher II*, 2007, personal work
→ *Ballet Dream*, 2008, Marie Claire, China
→→ *The Seventies are Back II*, 2008, personal work

TOOLS
Pen, paper, Adobe Illustrator, Adobe Photoshop, Wacom tablet

CLIENTS
BBDO, Heye & Partner, Publicis, Marie Claire China, Fit for Fun, Reader's Digest, Formes de Luxe, Rotkäppchen Sektkellerei, Hotel Pica Paca Gdansk

AGENT
Smart Magna
Athens, Greece
www.smartmagna.com

DieKleinert
Munich, Germany
www.diekleinert.de

Kyung Soon Park

1973 born in Kyung-Gi, South Korea | lives and works in Oakville, Ontario, Canada
www.levycreative.com

"I try to set the tone of the story being told. Everybody comes with their own unique set of preconceptions that I can alter, challenge, or reinforce."

„Ich versuche, auf die erzählte Geschichte einzustimmen. Jeder kommt mit eigenen vorgefassten Meinungen, die ich verändern, herausfordern oder verstärken kann."

« Je m'efforce de donner un ton à l'histoire qui est racontée. Chacun apporte sa propre batterie d'idées préconçues, que je peux ensuite modifier, questionner ou renforcer. »

↑   *Motivation*, 2008, Runner's World
→   *Frog Hunting*, 2007, selected for "The Best of Show from Creative Quarterly"
→→ *Adventures*, 2008, No Parachute Required

TOOLS
Ink, brush, Adobe Photoshop, Fabriano 140 lbs watercolour papers

CLIENTS
More, Runner's World, Oxford University Press, Report On Business, The Globe and Mail, Canadian Music Publishers Association, Editions Flammarion, Seattle Metropolitan magazine

SELECTED AWARDS
_ American Illustration 26
_ Society of Illustrators in Los Angeles
_ Creative Quarterly
_ 3x3 magazine Student Show

SELECTED EXHIBITIONS
_ Headlines, Sheridan Gad Show, 2007
_ Work & Life, Uppercase Gallery, 2008
_ No Parachute, Gallery 1313, 2008
_ Subtext TBA, 2009

AGENT
Levy Creative Management New York, USA
www.levycreative.com

↑ *Obsession*, 2007, personal work, featured in Creative Quarterly, Issue #10
↖ *Hands Across the Water*, 2008, More magazine
← *Standing Tall*, 2008, personal work, Creative Quarterly Professional Show "Gold Medal"

Dugald Stermer

1936 born in Los Angeles (CA), USA | lives and works in San Francisco (CA), USA
www.dugaldstermer.com

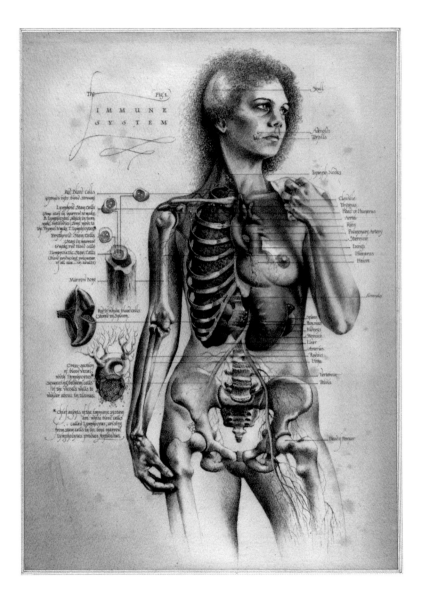

← *Langur*, 2006, personal work
→ *Bear Island*, 2000, Audubon magazine

TOOLS
Pencil, watercolour, coloured pencil

CLIENTS
Time, Esquire, The New York Times, The Washington Post, The New Yorker, GQ, Rolling Stone, The Los Angeles Times, Levi's, Iams Pet Food, The San Diego Zoo, Jaguar Motor Cars, BMW, Nike

SELECTED AWARDS
_ Art Directors Club New York
_ Society of Illustrators
_ Communication Arts Annuals

SELECTED EXHIBITIONS
_ Retrospective exhibition, California Academy of Sciences, 1986
_ Jernigan-Wicker Gallery, solo exhibition, San Francisco, 1996
_ Strybing Arboretum, 1999

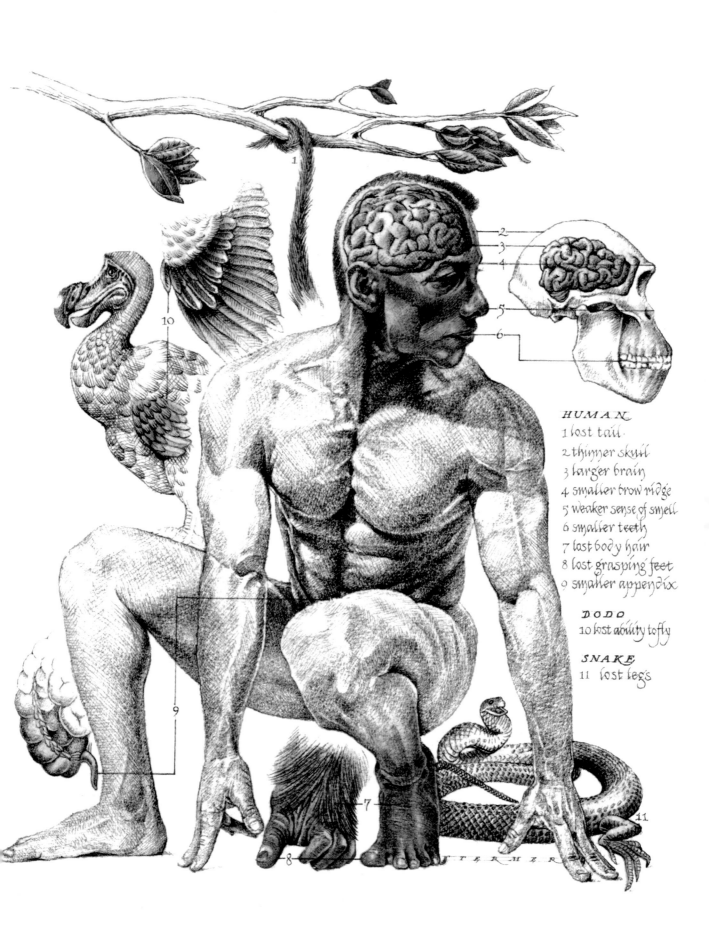

HUMAN
1 lost tail
2 thinner skull
3 larger brain
4 smaller brow ridge
5 weaker sense of smell
6 smaller teeth
7 lost body hair
8 lost grasping feet
9 smaller appendix

DODO
10 lost ability to fly

SNAKE
11 lost legs

Frank Stockton

1980 born in Santa Ana (CA), USA | lives and works in New York (NY), USA
www.frankstockton.com

"I love making pictures and telling stories. If I get to do those two things, everyone is happy."

„Ich liebe es, Bilder zu schaffen und Geschichten zu erzählen. Wenn ich solche Sachen machen darf, sind alle glücklich und zufrieden."

« J'aime dessiner et raconter des histoires. Si je parviens à faire les deux à la fois, tout le monde est content. »

↑ *Junkie*, 2007, Radar magazine
→ *Umberto Eco*, 2006, unpublished
→→ *Run!* 2008, Runner's World
↓↓ *Bad Blood*, 2007, Intelligence Report

TOOLS
Pen, ink, Adobe Photoshop

CLIENTS
Best Life, Businessweek, Entertainment Weekly, ESPN, Esquire, Fast Company, Forbes, Glamour, GQ, Intelligence Report, Men's Fitness, Men's Health, The New Yorker, Penthouse, Playboy, The Washington Post

SELECTED AWARDS
_ Society of Illustrators 51
_ Communication Arts Illustration Annual 49
_ American Illustration
_ ATA World Champion of Forms, 2000
_ Eastbluff Boys & Girls Club (Youth of the Year), 1994

SELECTED EXHIBITIONS
_ Society of Illustrators 51, 2009
_ Drawn To Expression (Phil Hayes Memorial show), Art Center College of Design, 2006
_ Love Sucks Love (Two-man show), Nucleus Gallery, 2006
_ Downright (collective exhibition), Pink Elephant Projects gallery, 2007
_ Le Crayon Brule (Two-man show), The Drawing Club, April 2006

← *Second Chances*, 2008, More magazine
→ *A Shot at Glory*, 2008, Penthouse
↓ *The Meeting*, 2008, Zeit magazine

Barron Storey

1940 born in Dallas (TX), USA | lives and works in San Francisco (CA), USA
www.barronstorey.com

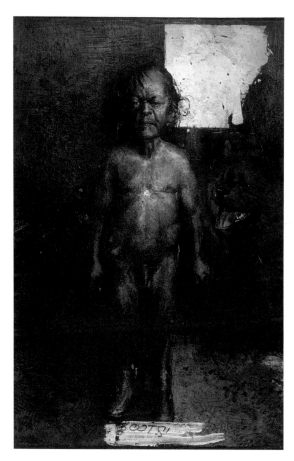

"I am a visual witness to the concerns of my society, from the informational to the subjective, deeply involved in teaching, and an advocate of documentation."

„Ich bin ein visueller Zeuge der Herausforderungen an meine Gesellschaft – vom Informellen bis zum Subjektiven. Ich bin beim Lehren höchst engagiert und ein Verfechter von Dokumentationen."

« Je suis un témoin visuel des préoccupations de ma société, de l'informationnel au subjectif ; je suis profondément engagé dans l'enseignement, et je défends la documentation. »

↑ *Boots*, magazine story illustration, 1975, Swank magazine
→ *Alexander Poniatoff Portrait*, 1998, American Heritage magazine, article: "10 People You Don't Know – That Changed Your Life"
→→ *Lord of the Flies*, book cover, 1980, Perigee Publishing

TOOLS
Pens, pencils, paints, acrylic media, photocopies, computer, found materials, urethane, string, rope (sculpture), photography

CLIENTS
National Geographic, Time, DC Comics, NASA, U.S. Information Agency, Graphic Novel Art, Franklin Library, Perigee Books, The New York Times, American Heritage, Sony, RCA Records, Stanford

SELECTED AWARDS
_ Society of Illustrators
_ Eisner Award (Comics)

SELECTED EXHIBITIONS
_ Black Iraq, Gallery Anno Domini, San Jose
_ U.S. Information Agency, Moscow
_ Osseus Labyrint Retrospective, Bert Green Gallery, Los Angeles
_ The Graphic Novel, Norman Rockwell Museum, Stockbridge, USA
_ Great Illustrators of Our Time, Rizzoli, New York

Studio Qube

2002 founded in Ontario, Canada | is Michael Chomicki & Cyprian Chomicki
www.studioqube.com

"We like to promote a critical mindset where we analyse work, rip it apart, and then start again anew."

„Unser Anliegen ist, kritische Einstellungen zu fördern, bei denen wir die Arbeiten analysieren, völlig auseinander nehmen und dann von Neuem beginnen."

« Nous prônons un état d'esprit critique qui consiste à analyser le travail, à laisser mûrir la chose, puis à recommencer de nouveau. »

↑ *Fantasy Football for Schools*, poster, 2007, The Independent
→ *Sport Battle*, 2008, personal work
→→ *Fade to Red*, 2007, personal work

TOOLS
Pencil, Adobe Illustrator, Adobe Photoshop

CLIENTS
Telegraph, Manchester United magazine, Future Publishing, Ballistic Publishing, SunScript

SELECTED EXHIBITIONS
_ International Manga Art Show, Fairfields Art Centre, UK

AGENT
Folio
London, UK
www.folioart.co.uk

Sugar Power

1997 founded in Zurich, Switzerland | based in Gisborne, Victoria, Australia
www.lintmuseum.com

↑ *Day of the Dead*, 2008, Que Pasa Newspaper
→ *Lascivious*, playing card deck, 2008, Lascivious Lingerie
→→ *San Miguel de Allende*, 2008, Que Pasa Newspaper

"What has struck me the most, throughout these experiences, is: if you follow what you love for a living you will be replete."

„Was mich während dieser Erfahrungen am tiefsten berührt hat: Wenn du das zum Lebensunterhalt machst, was du wirklich liebst, wirst du reich beschenkt."

« Voici ce qui m'a le plus frappé au cours de ces expériences : lorsqu'on fait ce qu'on aime comme profession, on est comblé. »

TOOLS
Mixed media, collage, digital tools

CLIENTS
DDB, Young & Rubicam, Leo Burnett, Saatchi & Saatchi, McCann Erickson, City of Melbourne, Telus, Volkswagen, Harper-Collins, Chevron, Time Out, The Times, The Telegraph, The Guardian, The Times (London)

SELECTED AWARDS
_ Advertising Awards, Montreux, Switzerland
_ Illustration of the Year, Create Awards, Melbourne, Australia

AGENT
Anna Goodson Management
Montreal, Canada
www.agoodson.com

Eye Candy
London, UK
www.eyecandy.co.uk

Creative Syndicate
Paris, France
www.creative-syndicate.com

Takeshi

1981 born in Saint Quentin, France | lives and works in New York (NY), USA

"Surreal and colorful compositions with a special emphasis on creative ideas and communication goals, and a very close attention to details."

„Hier mischen sich surreale und farbenprächtige Kompositionen, kreative Ideen und kommunikative Ziele bei sehr genauer Beachtung von Details."

« Des compositions surréelles et colorées, où l'accent est mis tout particulièrement sur les idées créatives et les objectifs de communication, avec un soin méticuleux pour les détails. »

↑   *Ins2one Streetwear*, advertising, 2008, Ins2one Streetwear
→   *Alstom*, 2009, Alstom
→→ *Electric Queen*, 2007. Photograph: Tor Kristensen

TOOLS
Adobe Illustrator, Adobe Photoshop, Corel Painter

CLIENTS
Toyota, Adidas, Swatch, MacLaren McCann, Advanced Photoshop, Young & Rubicam, Ferrero Rocher, EMI Music, Sony BMG, Knorr, TBWA Toronto, Exo7, BBDO Montreal, FPLQ, Suzuki, Unicef

SELECTED EXHIBITIONS
_ Ninkasi Kaos, Lyon, 2007
_ Little Soba, Saint Etienne, 2007

AGENT
Colagene
Montreal, Canada
Paris, France
www.colagene.com

Queen

Sharon Tancredi

1959 born in Chicago (IL), USA | lives and works in Brighton, UK
www.sharontancredi.com

"*Inspirations are many, from 15th-century Christian altar-pieces to 1950s packaging and design, American and Latin American folk art, street graphics, and all things kitsch!*"

„Die Inspirationen sind vielfältig – von christlichen Altären des 15. Jahrhunderts über Verpackung und Design der 1950er Jahre bis hin zu amerikanischer und lateinamerikanischer Volkskunst, Straßenmalereien und allem, was irgendwie nach Kitsch aussieht!"

« De nombreuses inspirations, des retables du XVe siècle au design et aux emballages des années 1950, en passant par le folklore américain et latino-américain, le graphisme urbain, et tout ce qui est kitsch ! »

↑ *Golden Goose*, children's book, 2008, Duncan Baird Publishing
Art Director: Suzanne Tuhrim
→ *Girl from Mars*, 2008, Little Black Dress Books
→→ *Mary of the Block*, 2007, self-promotion

TOOLS
Adobe Illustrator, Adobe Photoshop

CLIENTS
Arc, M&C Saatchi, McCann, Blue Marlin Brand Design, The Economist, The Independent, GQ magazine, Sky magazine, Duncan Baird Publishing, Harcourt Publishing, Hachette Book Group, Morgan Cain Publishing, Pearson Education

SELECTED AWARDS
_ 2004 The Association of Illustrators, Gold Award 2008
_ 3x3 magazine
_ The Association of Illustrators 2008
_ Creative Match Flair Illustrator of the Month 2008

SELECTED EXHIBITIONS
_ Association of Illustrators Images, UK, 2003, 2004, 2006, 2008
_ 3x3 magazine, Student Illustration Awards Exhibition, New York, 2003

AGENT
Folio
London, UK
www.folioart.co.uk

↑ *Green Machine*, 2005, Intelligent Life magazine,
Penny Garrett

→ *Masquerade Show*, 2008, R&R Partners,
Rio Hotel & Casino

← *Mother Nature*, 2008, Delta Sky magazine
Art Director: Ann Harvey

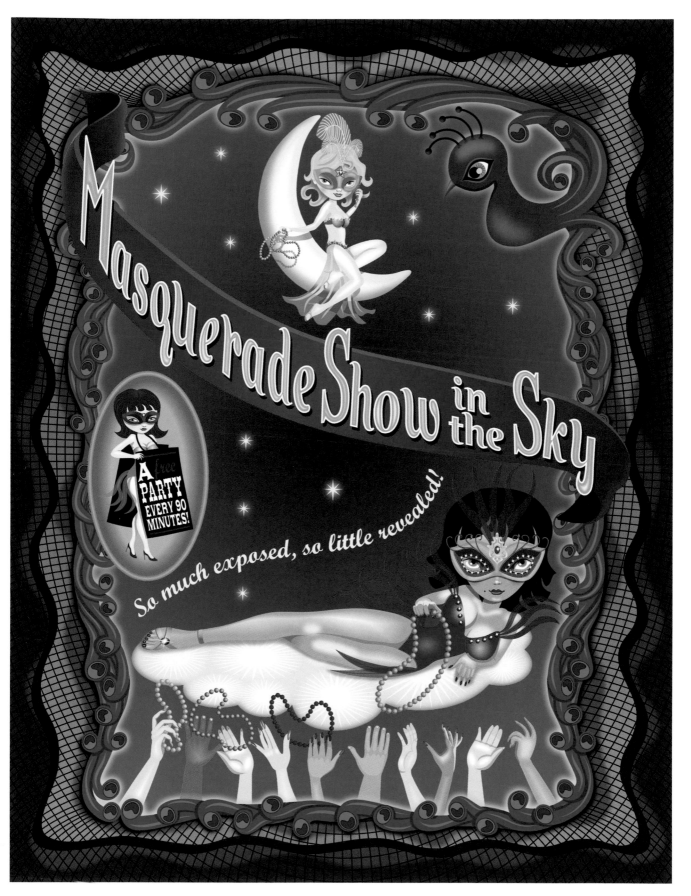

Jay Taylor

1983 born in Walsall, UK | lives and works in Stafford, UK
www.scribblejay.co.uk

"With social issues playing a big part in ideals, my style plays on life's little imperfections and is a big fan of the 'happy accident.'"

„Weil soziale Probleme bei Idealen eine große Rolle spielen, spielt mein Stil mit den kleinen Unzulänglichkeiten des Lebens und ist ein großer Fan des ,glücklichen Zufalls'. "

« Les questions sociales ayant pour moi un rôle majeur, idéologiquement parlant, mon style joue avec les petits aléas de la vie et affectionne l'‹ accident heureux ›. »

↑   *Gambling*, 2008, self-promotion
→   *Rock Climbing*, 2008, Continental magazine
    Art Director: Carolyne Bowes
→→ *Throw-Away Environment*, 2009, self-promotion

TOOLS
Hand drawings, computer

CLIENTS
The Guardian, Readers Digest, The Independent, Radio Times, Virgin, Channel 4, Royal Mail, Right Start, Times Education, JWT, Harcourt Courant, The Advocate, Out magazine, Nuvo magazine

SELECTED AWARDS
_ Association of Illustrators' Images Annual
_ Flair Illustrator Award, Creativematch

SELECTED EXHIBITIONS
_ New Arrivals, New Voices, Association of Illustrators, Coningsby Gallery
_ MUK (collective exhibtion), WSA collective.

AGENT
Anna Goodson Management
Quebec, Canada
www.agoodson.com

Agent Orange
London, UK
http://agentorange.co.uk

↑ *The Teenagers*, 2008, Mixmag magazine. Art Director: Hayden Russell
↗ *Global Warming*, Christmas promo, 2008, Anna Goodson Management
→ *Shooting Practice*, 2008, D magazine. Art Director: David Radabaugh

Team Hawaii

2001 founded in Stockholm, Sweden
www.teamhawaii.se

↑   *R.I.P.*, 2005, Stick
→   *Stureplan*, 2008, Appelbergs Publication

"A strong sense of humour and visual concepts, that's Team Hawaii!"

„Ein starker Sinn für Humor und ein gutes Gespür für visuelle Konzepte – das ist Team Hawaii!"

« Un solide sens de l'humour et du concept visuel, voilà le Team Hawaii ! »

TOOLS
Collage, digital camera,
Adobe Photoshop, paper,
pen, pencil, scissors

CLIENTS
Aftonbladet, Appelbergs,
Arla, Bonnier, Darling,
Gourmet, Habit, H & M,
LAVA, Moderna Tider, Neo

AGENT
NU Agency
Stockholm, Sweden
www.nuagency.se

Mike Terry

1947 born in Folkestone, UK | lives and works in Saltwood, UK

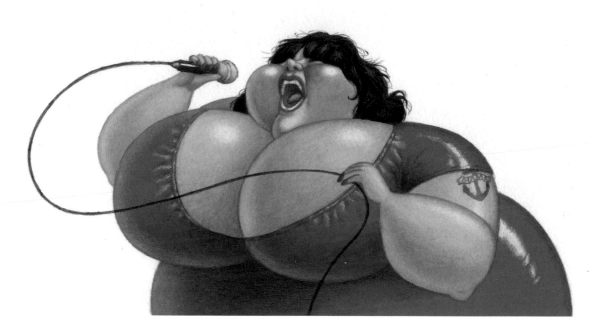

↑ *Beth Ditto*, 2008, self-promotion
→ *Pete Doherty*, 2008, self-promotion

"My work can be best described as 'humorous realism', and I endeavour to create
an image which could be cartoon in nature but is rendered as realistically as possible."

„Meine Arbeiten beschreibt man am besten mit dem Begriff ,humorvoller Realismus', und ich bemühe mich,
ein Bild zu schaffen, das von seiner Natur her ein Cartoon ist, aber so realistisch wie möglich dargestellt wird.“

« Les mots ‹réalisme humoristique› décrivent assez bien ce que je fais ; je tente de créer une image
de nature peut-être caricaturale, mais que je rends avec autant de réalisme que possible. »

TOOLS	CLIENTS	SELECTED AWARDS	SELECTED EXHIBITIONS	AGENT
Gouache, coloured pencil, pastels	JWT, Young & Rubicam, Ogilvy & Mather, McBains, The Economist, Golf Monthly, The Times, The Mail on Sunday, Bloomsbury Children's Books, Penguin Children's Books, Little Tiger Press, Reader's Digest	_ D&AD Illustration awards _ Mecanorma Award	_ Association of Illustrators Images _ A Retrospective, Association of Illustrators Images, Gallery One	Folio London, UK www.folioart.co.uk

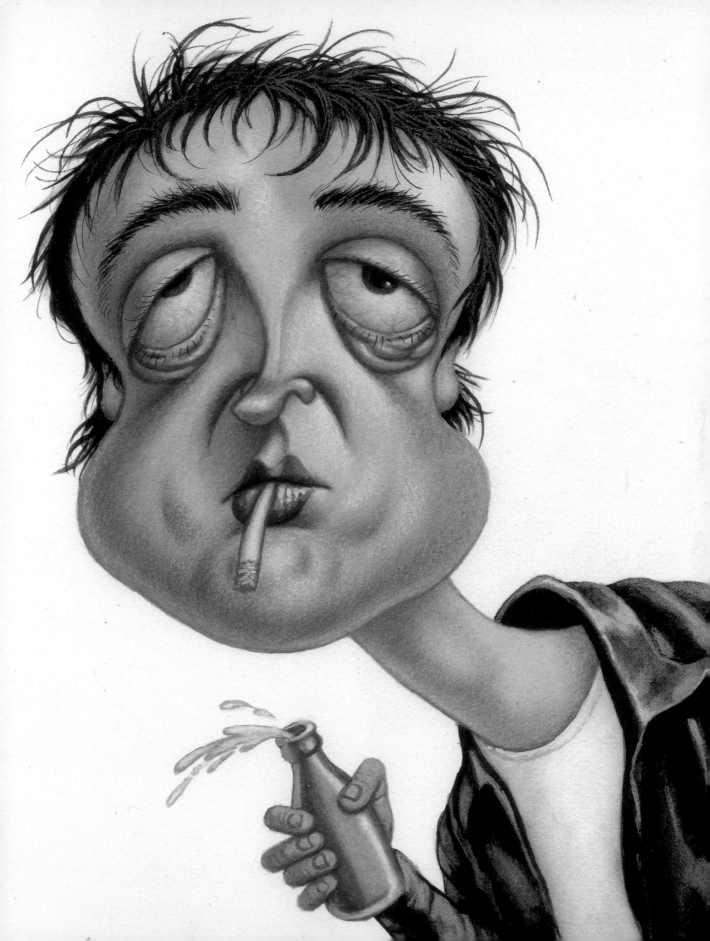

Alex Trochut

1981 born in Barcelona, Spain | lives and works in Barcelona, Spain
www.alextrochut.com

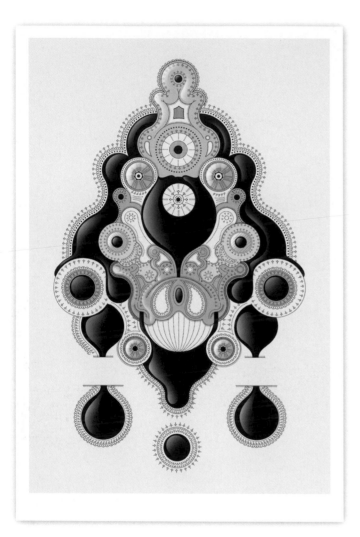

"More is More."

„More is More."

« Plus, c'est plus. »

↑ *Music Loves You*, poster and laser engraved MP3 player, 2008, Zune Originals
→ *10 ways to get a job*, 2008, Computer Arts
→→ *Type-Soul*, cover, 2008, XFUNS magazine

TOOLS
Pencil, Adobe Freehand,
Adobe Illustrator, Adobe
Photoshop, Wacom tablet

CLIENTS
Adidas, BBH, Burton, British
Airways, Coca-Cola, Converse,
Johnnie Walker, ING, Fallon,
Puig, Group, Nike, Nixon,
Saatchi & Saatchi, Sixpack,
The Rolling Stones, The New
York Times, Zune

SELECTED AWARDS
_ TDC 2005 Award of
Exellence Display Type
_ Communication Arts 2008
Certificate of Excellence
_ ADC 2008 Young Guns

SELECTED EXHIBITIONS
_ Beautiful Decay, Issue Z
_ If you Could, 2008
_ Resist!
_ Ink This
_ Now Showing

AGENT
DebutArt
London, UK
www.debutart.com

Illustrissimo
Paris, France
www.illustrissimo.com

Levine and Leavitt
New York, USA
www.llreps.com

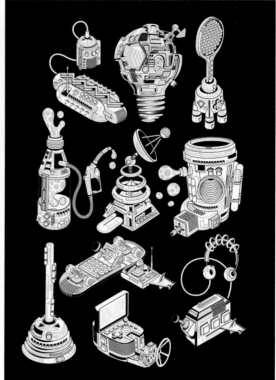

↑ ↘ *Humans Are Dead*, glow in the dark T-shirts, 2008, Sixpack
←   *Cultura Urbana*, poster, 2007, Cultura Urbana Hip Hop festival,
    in collaboration with Inocuo the sign

← *Rolled Gold +*, CD and vinyl cover, 2007,
The Rolling Stones
→ *2008*, cover and article illustration, 2008,
The Guardian G2
↓ *Attractive Numbers*, print advertising
campaign, 2008, British Airways, BBH UK

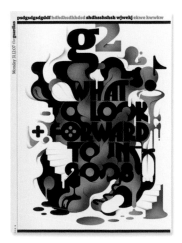

Fuco Ueda

1979 born in Tochigi, Japan | lives and works in Tokyo, Japan
www.geocities.jp/uedafuco

↑ *Symbiosis 4, Slime mould*, 2007, personal work
→ *Symbiosis 1, Toadstool*, 2007, personal work

"My work is accompanied by a feeling of strange floating, and invites you to enter a different chaotic world."

„Meine Arbeit wird von einem eigenartigen Gefühl des Strömens und Fließens begleitet und lädt alle ein, in eine ganz andere, chaotische Welt einzutauchen."

« Accompagné d'un étrange sentiment de flottement, mon travail vous invite à pénétrer dans un monde différent et chaotique. »

TOOLS	CLIENTS	SELECTED AWARDS	SELECTED EXHIBITIONS		AGENT
Acrylic, shell powder on canvas	Gallery Kogure	_ TIS Public Advertisement 2002	_ Solo exhibition, Secret Garden, Tokyo, 2006	_ Ephemera Exhibition, Los Angeles, 2007	Gallery Kogure Tokyo, Japan
		_ The 16ᵗʰ Graphic Arts Hitothubo Ten	_ Solo exhibition, Aquarium Dreamy, Tokyo, 2007	_ Esao Andrews and Fuco Ueda, Seattle, 2008	www.g-kogure.ecweb.jp
		_ VOCA Exhibition 2004	_ Solo exhibition, Symbiosis, Tokyo, 2008		
		_ Japan Visual Art Exhibition			

↑   *Elevator Hall*, 2007, personal work
→   *Twilight Zone 2*, 2007, personal work
↓   *Panorama visual hallucination (the right side)*, 2007, personal work

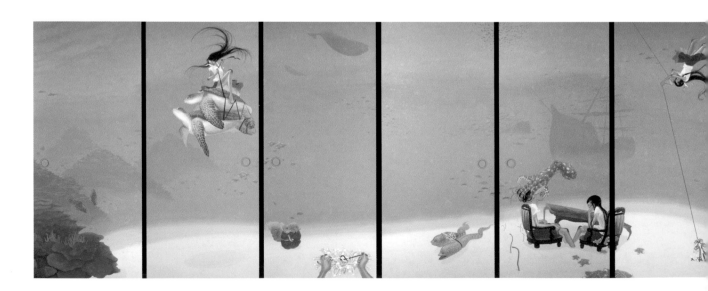

↑　*Mebae 1*, 2008, personal work
↗　*Mebae 2*, 2008, personal work
↘　*Small Friend 4*, 2008, personal work

↑　*Yume No Kayoizi*, 2008, personal work
↗　*Hana No Yume*, 2008, personal work
↘　*Small Friend 1*, 2008, personal work

Amanda Visell

1978 born in Puyallup (WA), USA | lives and works in Pasadena (CA), USA
www.amandavisell.com

↑   *Bayou-hoo*, 2007, personal work
→   *Pegaphunt*, 2008, personal work

"I paint what I find in the sock drawer of my brain. Sometimes you find a sock with no match, sometimes you find 20 bucks."

„Ich male, was ich in der Sockenschublade meines Hirns finde: manchmal eine einzelne Socke, manchmal auch 20 Dollar."

« Je peins ce que je trouve dans le tiroir à chaussettes de mon cerveau. Parfois j'en tire une chaussette dépareillée, parfois un billet de 20 dollars. »

TOOLS

Cel-vinyl acrylic paint, board, wood

CLIENTS

Disneyland, Kidrobot, Munky King, Strange Co, Laika, Fortune magazine, Real Simple magazine, Bust magazine, Portland Mercury

SELECTED EXHIBITIONS

_ Tic Toc Apocalypse solo exhibition, M Modern Gallery, Palm Springs, 2008
_ Switcheroo solo exhibition, Gallery 1988, Los Angeles, 2007

_ Pirates of the Caribbean Anniversary, Disneyland California, 2008
_ Peter Pan Anniversary, Disneyland California, 2008
_ I Am 8 Bit Group Show, Los Angeles, 2006

← *Honeymoon is over*, 2006, personal work
→ *Poopicorn brigade*, 2008, personal work
↙ *Jackalope*, 2008, personal work
↓ *Wood dragon and the termites*, 2008, personal work

Marco Wagner

1982 born in Würzburg, Germany | lives and works in Höchberg, Germany
www.marcowagner.net

↑   *Untitled*, 2008, Effilee, magazine article "Fit durch Fett"
→   *Übung #3*, 2008, Horncastle Verlag
→→ *Zwei/1*, 2008, personal work

TOOLS
Pen, pencil, paper, boards, cardboards, acrylic, crayons, Adobe Photoshop

CLIENTS
Bajazzo Verlag, Büchergilde Gutenberg, Deutsche Akademie für Kinder- und Jugendliteratur, Effilee Magazin, Jung von Matt, Murphy Design, Playboy Germany, Wirtschaftswoche

SELECTED AWARDS
_ 3x3 magazine
_ Communication Arts Illustration Competition 49
_ European Design Awards 2008

SELECTED EXHIBITIONS
_ Superhero Exhibition, San Diego, 2008
_ Solo exhibition, Galerie Mari Jo, Volkach
_ Artkollision II, Würzburg, 2008
_ Know exhibition, Gen Art's Vanguard, Miami, 2008
_ One Night Show, Damen und Herren, Düsseldorf

AGENT
Jutta Fricke
Münster, Germany
www.jutta-fricke.de

↑ *Bill Wyman*, 2008, Playboy Germany
   Art Director: Wolfgang Buß
→ *Ludwig II*, 2009, Playboy Germany
   Art Director: Wolfgang Buß

↑ *Johnny Cash*, 2008, Playboy Germany
  Art Director: Wolfgang Buß
→ *Walt Disney*, 2009, Playboy Germany
  Art Director: Wolfgang Buß

Silke Werzinger

1983 born in Weißenburg, Germany | lives and works in Nürnberg, Germany

*"I like pictures you can discover
step by step, pictures which
tell a story, pictures that cause
a reaction, hopefully a smile."*

„Mir gefallen Bilder, die man Stück für Stück entdecken
kann, die eine Geschichte erzählen, Bilder, die eine
Reaktion hervorrufen - und hoffentlich ein Lächeln."

« J'aime les images qu'on peut découvrir petit à petit,
les images qui racontent une histoire, les images
qui provoquent une réaction, de préférence un sourire. »

↑   *Healing with Sound*, 2008, Brigitte Balance magazine
→   *London Calling*, T-shirt, 2008, Undiz
→→ *64 things a woman should have done in life*, 2008, Annabelle magazine

---

TOOLS
Hand drawing, mixed media

CLIENTS
Die Zeit Campus, Brigitte, Neon, Nylon magazine, DDB, Peugeot, Publicis, Annabelle, Maxi, Tush, Dogs, Indie magazine, Time Out New York, WAD magazine, Glamour magazine

SELECTED AWARDS
_ Red Dot Design Award 2008
_ Art Directors Club Germany 2008
_ DDC Gute Gestaltung 09

SELECTED EXHIBITIONS
_ Red Dot Winner's Exhibition, Red Dot Design Museum, 2008
_ Showroom Opening, Onkel&Onkel Verlag, Berlin, 2008
_ Designers' Night, Nuremberg, 2007

AGENT
Colagene
Montreal, Canada
Paris, France
www.colagene.com

Phil Wheeler

1972 born in Jersey, UK | lives and works in Cadiz, Spain
www.philwheelerillustrations.com

← *Possibility Landscape*, desktop wallpaper,
2007, Budweiser/Flavorpill campaign
→ *Waterfall*, advertising, 2008,
Saatchi & Saatchi NY, New York State
Tourist Board campaign

*"Perfectionist tendencies and an early love affair with vectors meant
I was drawn to the digital. Despite the vector style, I usually work in pixels."*

*„Meine perfektionistischen Tendenzen und eine frühe Liebesaffäre mit Vektoren führten dazu,
dass ich mich zum Digitalen hingezogen fühlte. Trotz des Vektorstils arbeite ich normalerweise mit Pixeln."*

*« Une tendance au perfectionnisme et une histoire d'amour précoce pour les vecteurs
m'ont voué au numérique. Malgré le style vectoriel, je travaille ordinairement avec des pixels. »*

TOOLS
Wacom tablet, Adobe
Photoshop, Adobe Illustrator

CLIENTS
Adidas, Adobe, IBM, Pepsi,
New York State Tourism Board,
Universal Music, Budweiser,
Pontiac

AGENT
Anna Goodson Management
Montreal, Canada
www.agoodson.com

↑   *Dance Grooves 1*, CD cover, 2008, Universal Music, commissioned by Peter Chadwick, Popular UK
←   *Dance Grooves 2*, CD cover, 2008, Universal Music, commissioned by Peter Chadwick, Popular UK

Nick White

1981 born in Cheltenham, UK | lives and works in London, UK
www.thisisnickwhite.com

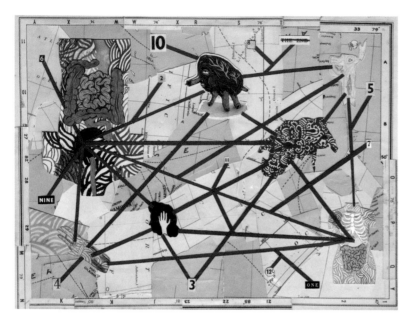

↑   *Inside out, Upside down*, 2009, Cent magazine
→   *Journal of a Collector*, 2008, World of Interiors magazine
→→ *Look Left Look Right*, 2008, personal work

> *"My work is characterised by pattern, collage, and a whole lot of heads. Which is lucky because I like pattern, collage, and a whole lot of heads."*

> „Meine Arbeiten werden durch Muster, Collagen und viele Köpfe charakterisiert. Das ist ein Glück, denn mir gefallen Muster, Collagen und viele Köpfe."

> « Mon travail se caractérise par les motifs, les collages, et toutes sortes de têtes. Ça tombe bien, j'aime les motifs, les collages et toutes sortes de têtes. »

TOOLS
Pen, pencils, felt tips, ink, gouache, found paper, imagery, screenprint ink, scalpel, glue

CLIENTS
Time Out London, World of Interiors, Plan B magazine, Cent magazine, NoBrow, Decode Media, Iron Man Records, Gronland Records

SELECTED EXHIBITIONS
_ Sale, The Royal Standard, Liverpool
_ The Joyful Bewilderment, Rough Trade East, London
_ Mystery Spot, Indos, London
_ Gutes Von Freunden, Frankfurt
_ Noise Festival, Liverpool Biennial, Liverpool, 2008

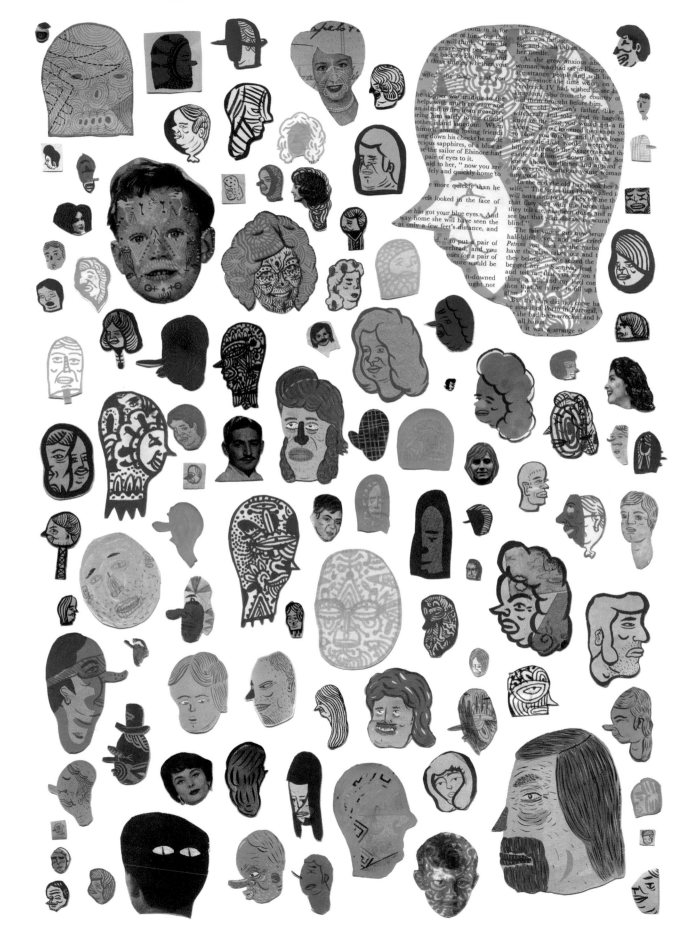

Autumn Whitehurst

1973 born in Providence (RI), USA | lives and works in Providence (RI), New Orleans (LA), and Brooklyn (NY), USA
www.art-dept.com/illustration/whitehurst

"My work is a clean combination of vector graphics and detailed rendering. I'm partial to less-is-more, though only in my work."

„Meine Arbeit ist eine saubere Kombination von Vektorgrafik und detailliertem Rendering. Ich lege es teilweise auf ‚weniger ist mehr' an, allerdings nur in meiner Arbeit."

« Mon travail est une nette combinaison d'images vectorielles et de rendu détaillé. J'ai un faible pour le précepte ‹moins, c'est plus›, mais dans le travail uniquement. »

↑   *Heat*, 2006, Las Vegas Weekly
→   *Sugar & Skin*, 2007, London Telegraph
→→ *Aguilera*, 2007, Tu Ciudad

TOOLS
Adobe Photoshop, Adobe
Illustrator, Corel Painter

CLIENTS
Diet Coke, Sapporo, Ray Ban,
Ecko Red, LeSportSac, Neiman
Marcus, Vogue Italia, British
Elle, Style.com

AGENT
Art Department
New York, USA
www.art-dept.com

↑   *Wish You Were Here*, 2004, Art Department, promotional

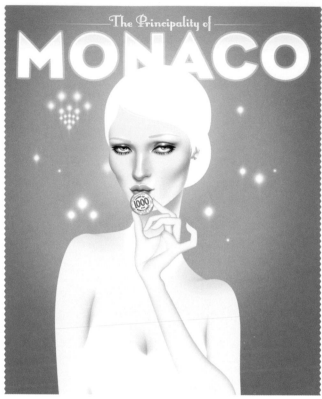

Monaco–It's just a Game, advertising, 2007, Greenteam For Monaco
→ *Sun*, 2007, London Telegraph
↓ *Kate and Pete*, 2007, London Telegraph

Steve Wilson

1979 born in Brighton, UK | lives and works in Brighton, UK
www.wilson2000.com

"Somewhere between
Psychedelia and Pop Art."

„Irgendwas zwischen
psychedelisch und Pop Art."

« Quelque part entre
le Psychédélique et le Pop Art. »

← *Man with Pipe*, 2007, personal work
→ *The Dongle*, 2008, 3 Mobile, Don't Panic Media

TOOLS
Paint, pencil, playdo, photocopiers, scanning, Adobe Photoshop, Adobe Illustrator

CLIENTS
MTV, Virgin, Julien MacDonald, Levi's, NYCGO, Coca-Cola, Wallpaper magazine, Nike, Vodafone, Neiman Marcus, Island Records, The Fader, Jalouse

SELECTED AWARDS
_ Creative Reviews, Creative Futures, Runner Up

SELECTED EXHIBITIONS
_ 100 pieces of Havana, Dray Walk Gallery, 2008

AGENT
Breed
London, UK
www.breedlondon.com

↑↑ *NYCGO Hot Dog*, 2008, BBH New York, NYCGO
↑   *NYCGO Sneaker*, 2008, BBH New York, NYCGO

↑↑ *Bullet For My Valentine*, personal work
↑   *Bird*, 2008, Sam Sparro, Island Records

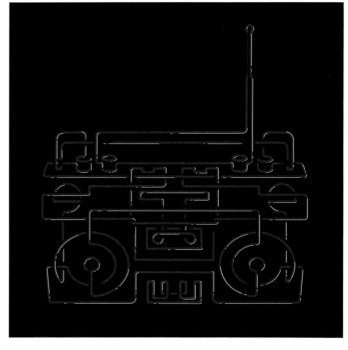

↑   *Sam Sparro portrait*, 2008, Sam Sparro, Island Records
→   *Neon Radio*, 2009, personal work

Jasper Wong

1983 born in Honolulu, Hawaii, USA | lives and works in Chi Fu Fa Yuen, Hong Kong
www.jasperwong.net

↑ *Twenty Four Inch Pythons*, 2008, personal work
→ *Nerds and Squares*, 2008, personal work
→→ *Pitiful Fool*, 2008, personal work

*"Cartoons and candy corn
and hairy old seventies porn,
that's what illustrators are made of."*

„*Cartoons und Candy Corn und behaarte alte
Pornos aus den Siebzigern – das ist der Stoff,
aus dem Illustratoren sind.*"

« *Dessins animés, candy corn et porno
poilu de la fin des années 70… l'étoffe dont sont
faits les illustrateurs.* »

TOOLS
Acrylic, gouache, canvas,
wood, Adobe Photoshop,
Adobe Illustrator, Wacom
tablet, paper, vellum, pencil,
pen, paint markers

CLIENTS
Crispin, Porter & Bogusky,
Mullen, DC shoes,
Zakkamono, Jackie Chan

SELECTED EXHIBITIONS
_ Pitiful Fools Solo Show,
Subtext, San Diego, USA
_ Kitsch Catch, Maison Folie
Wazemmes, Lille, France
_ Plushform, Rotofugi Gallery,
Chicago, USA
_ Kicks, Subtext, San Diego,
USA

_ Superhero Shenanigans, Red
Ink, San Francisco, USA

Wilfrid Wood

1968 born in London, UK | lives and works in London, UK
www.wilfridwood.com

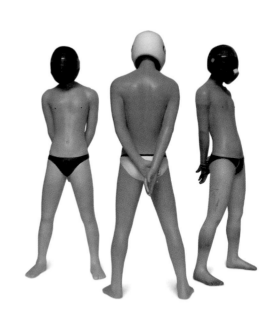

"I am inspired by friends, legs, eyes, animals, lips, ice cream, toys, transvestites, cartoons, teeth, bottoms, fashion, sport, freaky dancers."

„Mich inspirieren Freunde, Beine, Augen, Tiere, Lippen, Eiscreme, Spielzeug, Transvestiten, Cartoons, Zähne, Hintern, Mode, Sport und abgefahrene Tänzer."

« Les amis, les jambes, les yeux, les animaux, les lèvres, les glaces, les jouets, les travestis, les bandes dessinées, les dents, les fesses, la mode, les sports, les danseurs zarbis, voilà ce qui m'inspire. »

↑   *Kluge*, 2007, Faber & Faber
→   *Dirty Bikers*, 2008, self-promotion
→→ *Characters*, 2007, self-promotion

TOOLS
Polymer clay, enamel paint

CLIENTS
Levi's, Fab, Publicis, Frosty Fruits, Amplify, Barclays, Howies, Faber & Faber, Puma, Philippe Starck

AGENT
Dutch Uncle
London, UK
www.dutchuncle.co.uk

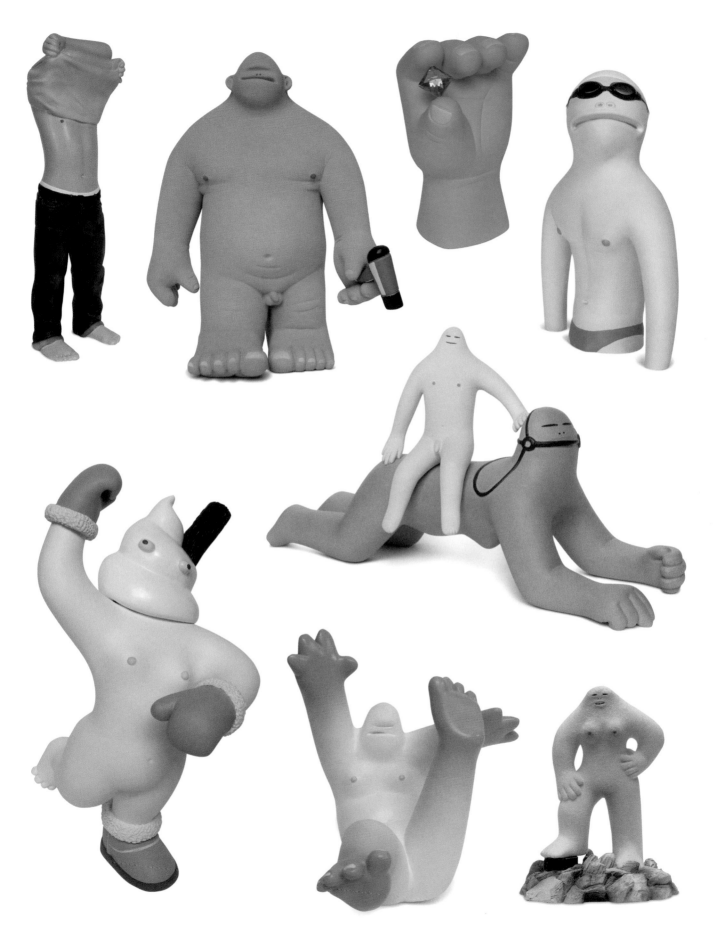

Matthew Woodson

1983 born in Bloomington (IN), USA | lives and works in Chicago (IL), USA
www.ghostco.org

"I use traditional, out-dated techniques and motifs to describe modern themes. Using natural imagery to convey the subtle emotions of the everyday."

„Ich verwende traditionelle, veraltete Techniken und Motive, mit denen ich moderne Themen beschreibe. Über natürliche Bilder will ich die subtilen Emotionen des Alltäglichen vermitteln."

« J'utilise des techniques et des motifs traditionnels et désuets pour exposer des questions actuelles. Je recours aux images naturelles pour communiquer les émotions subtiles du quotidien. »

↑   *Untitled*, 2009, personal work
→   *Untitled*, 2006, personal work
→→ *Untitled*, 2007, Penthouse magazine

TOOLS
Brush, quill, ink, watercolour, Wacom tablet, Adobe Photoshop

CLIENTS
The Boston Globe, Business Week, Chicago magazine, ESPN magazine, The Folio Society, Forbes magazine, Glamour magazine, Penthouse magazine, Perry Ellis, Wired, Random House, Scholastic, Type Records, UNICEF

AGENT
Art Department
New York, USA
www.art-dept.com

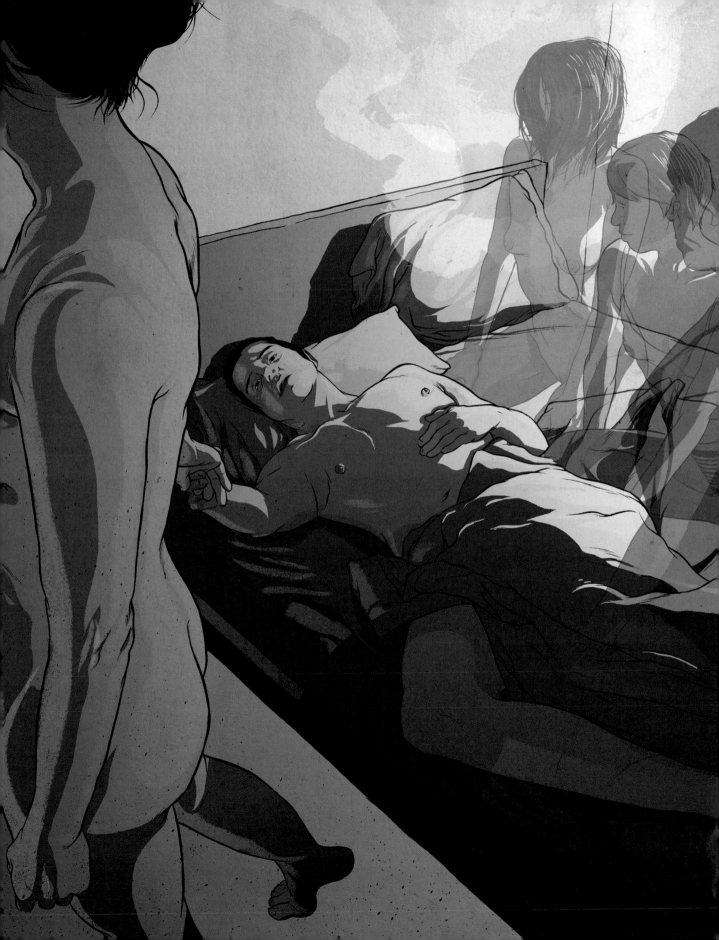

↑   *And Suddenly I Miss Everyone*, 2007, personal work
→   *Untitled*, 2008, Art Department, based on Wong Kar Wai's
      "In The Mood For Love" for a promotional book
↓   *And Though You Have Loved a Thousand Men*, 2007, personal work

Yiorgos Yiacos

1978 born in Athens, Greece | lives and works in Athens, Greece
www.twelvetimestwo.com

↑   *Damn You (Mr. Stanton)*, 2006, The Poor magazine
→   *The Solution Was Obvious*, 2006, personal work
→→ *Cramps Tribute*, 2007, personal work

"An illustration is never good enough unless I have something to say. I put in my views on society, on people, my wants, likes, and dislikes."

„Eine Illustration ist nie gut genug, wenn ich nichts zu sagen habe. Ich lege meine Ansichten über Gesellschaft, Leute, meine Bedürfnisse, Neigungen und Abneigungen hinein."

« Une illustration n'est bonne que si j'ai quelque chose à dire. J'y mets ce que je pense de la société, des gens, ce que je désire, ce qui me plaît et me déplaît. »

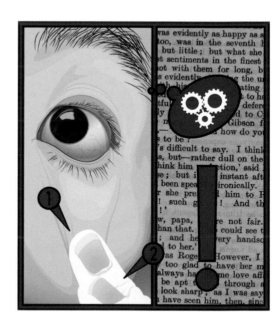

TOOLS
Adobe Illustrator, Adobe Photoshop, pencil, digital camera, Wacom tablet, found imagery

CLIENTS
Kathimerini Publications, Daphne Publications

SELECTED AWARDS
_EVGE Greek Awards for Graphic Design & Illustration 2005/2006/2008

SELECTED EXHIBITIONS
_DesignWalk, Athens, 2008/2007
_Re:Cover, Yiomisti Kefali Gallery, Sifnos Island, 2007
_Green Design, Athens, 2008
_Mapping Europe, Athens, 2007

AGENT
Smart Magna
Athens, Greece
www.smartmagna.com

Damyeong Yoo-Hartlaub

1979 born in Seoul, South Korea | lives and works in Büttelborn, Germany
www.damyeong.de

> "I mix two and three dimensions with paper-cutting and folding techniques to create new textures. I express a feeling of poetic paradox using decorative methods."

> „Ich vermische durch Papierschnitte und Falttechniken Zwei- und Dreidimensionalität, um neue Texturen und Oberflächen zu schaffen. Ich vermittle ein Gefühl fürs poetisch Paradoxe durch dekorative Methoden.“

> « Je mêle deux ou trois dimensions avec des découpages et des pliages, pour créer de nouvelles textures. J'exprime un sentiment de paradoxe poétique à l'aide de méthodes décoratives. »

↑ *Headache*, 2008, personal work, nominated for Illustrative Young Award 2008
→ *La nuit blanche l'aube noire*, CD design, 2008, Tyle Music
→→ *La nuit blanche l'aube noire*, CD design, 2008, Tyle Music

---

TOOLS
Pencil, paper cutting, digital camera, crayon, Adobe Photoshop

CLIENTS
Les Arènes, Tyle Music

SELECTED AWARDS
_Illustrative Young Award 2008 (nomination)

SELECTED EXHIBITIONS
_Illustrative, Zurich, 2008

Jaime Zollars

1997 born in Arlington (VA), USA | lives and works in Baltimore (MD), USA
www.jaimezollars.com

"I strive to create images that are accessible, narrative, and a bit subversive. I like to present heavier subjects (like war, death, and environmental destruction) in alternate realities, where new and less biased perspectives can be gleaned."

„Mein Bestreben ist, Bilder zu schaffen, die zugänglich, erzählend und ein wenig subversiv sind. Mir gefällt es, schwerwiegende Themen wie Krieg, Tod und Umweltzerstörung in alternativen Realitäten zu präsentieren, aus denen man neue und nicht so tendenzielle Perspektiven herauslesen kann."

« J'aspire à créer des images accessibles, narratives et un peu subversives. J'aime traiter les sujets difficiles (la guerre, la mort et la destruction de l'environnement, par exemple) dans des réalités alternatives, où des perspectives nouvelles et moins partiales peuvent être glanées. »

← *Garden Secret*, 2006, personal work, Black Maria Gallery
→ *Red Bird Battalion*, 2008, personal work, Copro Nason Gallery

---

TOOLS
Collage, acrylic paint

CLIENTS
United Airlines, American Red Cross, L.A. Weekly, Tricycle Books, Clarion Books, Scholastic, Marshall Cavendish, Cricket Publications

SELECTED AWARDS
_ Society of Illustrators Los Angeles
_ 3x3 magazine
_ National Conference of The Society of Children's Book Writers and Illustrators
_ Spectrum Annuals
_ Illustration West

SELECTED EXHIBITIONS
_ Melancholia solo exhibition, Copro Nason Gallery, Los Angeles
_ Systema Naturae: Submerged, Gallery Nucleus, Los Angeles
_ Systema Naturae, Gallery Nucleus, Los Angeles
_ Far Far Away solo exhibition, Lunar Boy Gallery, Astoria, USA
_ Charm and Menace, Black Maria Gallery, Los Angeles

AGENT
Christina A. Tugeau Williamsburg, USA
www.catugeau.com

← *Tengu Graveyard*, 2008,
   personal work, Gallery Nucleus
↗ *Stirring*, 2007, personal work
→ *Between Scylla*, 2008,
   personal work, Gallery Nucleus
↓ *Pink Elephant Procession*, 2007,
   personal work, Lunar Boy Gallery

Acknowledgements / Danksagungen / Remerciements

First and foremost, my sincere thanks go to all the illustrators for supplying the most astonishing work and for constantly keeping in touch with us in order to improve the end result. After years of technological improvement, they have demonstrated that not only is illustration important, it is something we find that we love more every day. My other big thanks, of course, go to Daniel Siciliano Bretas, my right hand at the headquarters in Cologne. Daniel worked tirelessly on the design and layout, paying meticulous attention to detail and delivering the final proofs in record time. I would also like to express my sincere gratitude to Steven Heller, who worked closely with us to select a truly diverse showcase of creative talent. His expertise as both editor and academic made it truly important for this publication, and his vast knowledge of illustration is unsurpassed. On our production front, Stefan Klatte has done an amazing job from beginning to end. Through his valiant efforts we were, as always, able to optimize each step of the production process, improving the quality along the way. I would also like to acknowledge all the illustrators' agents, who were always on hand to lend us their support.

Julius Wiedemann

Imprint

© 2009 TASCHEN GmbH
Hohenzollernring 53, D-50672 Köln
www.taschen.com

To stay informed about upcoming TASCHEN titles,
please request our magazine at www.taschen.com/magazine
or write to TASCHEN, Hohenzollernring 53, D-50672 Cologne,
Germany, contact@taschen.com, Fax: +49-221-254919.
We will be happy to send you a free copy of our magazine
which is filled with information about all of our books.

Page 006: *Diamond*, 2008, by Hans Christian Oren for Oh Yeah Studio
Pages 016–017: *Mother Nature's Son One*, 2005, by Cathie Bleck
Page 446: *Dream Machine*, 2007, by Nik Ainley

Design and layout: Daniel Siciliano Bretas
Production: Stefan Klatte

Editor: Julius Wiedemann
Editorial Coordination: Daniel Siciliano Bretas and Jutta Hendricks

French Translation: Martine Joulia, Equipo de Edición
German Translation: Jürgen Dubau

Printed in Italy
ISBN 978–3–8365–1487–3